Further Communication Strategies

by David Paul

THOMSON

Australia • Canada • Mexico • Singapore • Spain • United Kingdom • United States

Further Communication Strategies
by David Paul

Publishing Director: Paul Tan
ELT Director: John Lowe
Senior Development Editor: Guy de Villiers
Marketing Manager: Ian Martin

ELT Consultant: Mark Rossiter
Interior/Cover Design: Lynn Dennett
Illustrator: Ross Thomson
Printer: Seng Lee Press

For more information, contact Thomson Learning, 5 Shenton Way, #01-01 UIC Building, Singapore 068808. Or you can visit our Internet site at http://www.thomsonlearningasia.com

The publisher would like to thank The Kobal Collection for their permission to reproduce photographs:
8: Made in America - Warner Bros, ph: Zade Rosenthal; 14: The Bourne Identity - Hypnotic/Universal, ph: Egon Endrenyi; 20: At the Circus - MGM; 26: Dead Poets Society - Touchstone, ph: Francois Duhamel; 32: Keystone Cops - Sennett Films; 38: Sound of Music - 20th Century Fox; 44: Independence Day - 20th Century Fox; 50: Waterloo - De Laurentiis/Mosfilm; 56: Erin Brockovich - Universal, ph: Bob Marshak; 62: Out of Africa - Universal, ph: Frank Connor; 68: Ali - Columbia, ph: Frank Connor; 74: The American President - Castle Rock/Universal/Wildwood, ph: Francois Duhamel; 80: Rogue Trader - Capitol, ph: Paul Chedlow; 86: Always - Universal, ph: Gary Graver; 92: Casino Royale - Columbia

For permission to use the material from this text or product, contact us by
Tel: (65) 6410-1200
Fax: (65) 6410-1208
Email: tlsg.info@thomson.com

ISBN 981-243-020-2

Printed in Singapore
2 3 4 5 6 07 06 05 04

Acknowledgments

I would like to thank:

Everyone at Thomson for their encouragement and belief in the project, especially Guy de Villiers, the development editor, and John Lowe, for recognizing the potential of the course.

Lynn Dennett for the wonderful design and so much hard work.

Brian Elliot and Lynn Dennett for the photographs, and the David English House staff who bravely volunteered to be models.

All those who encouraged this project in the early stages, especially Yvonne de Henseler, Vaughan Jones, Richard Kemp and Mike Esplen.

All the staff and teachers who have been part of David English House in Hiroshima, Seoul and Bangkok over the years. Thank you so much for your support and hard work.

In addition, we would like to extend our thanks to the professionals who have offered invaluable comments and suggestions during the development of the course. Many thanks to those listed below:

David Paul

Carol Rinnert	Hiroshima City University, Hiroshima, Japan
Susan Lee	Lykeion Language Forum, Seoul, South Korea
Alice Svendson	Jumonji Women's College, Tokyo, Japan
Sangdo Woo	Gongju National University of Education, Gongju, South Korea
Michael Guest	Miyazaki Medical College, Miyazaki, Japan
Grace Chang	Tak-Ming Technical College, Taipei, Taiwan
Rob Waring	Notre Dame Seishin University, Okayama, Japan
Michael Wiener	SIAM Computer & Language Institute, Bangkok, Thailand
Kerry Muir	Tokai University Junior College, Tokyo, Japan
Bill Pellowe	Kinki University, Fukuoka, Japan
Sophia Shang	Whatcom College, Bellingham, USA
Jason Kim	BCM Language Institute, Seoul, South Korea
Renee Sawazaki	Rikkyo University, Tokyo, Japan
Stephen Shrader	LIOJ, Odawara, Japan
Professor Kyung-Whan Cha	Chung-Ang University, Seoul, South Korea
Kevin Sawatzky	Nova Futamatagawa School, Kanagawa, Japan
Anne-Marie Hadzima	National Taiwan University, Taipei, Taiwan
Simon Howell	Kansai Gaidai, Osaka, Japan
Linh Thuy Pallos	Kyoto Tachibana Women's University, Kyoto, Japan
David Campbell	JOY Academy, Hokkaido, Japan
Professor Oryang Kwon	Seoul National University, Seoul, South Korea
Michael Bradley	Bradley's English School, Koriyama City, Japan
Thomas Asada Grant	Daito Bunka University, Saitama, Japan
Chia Jung Tang	National Chengchi University, Taipei, Taiwan
Bob Jones	REJ English House, Gifu, Japan
Joseph Wang	Southern Taiwan University of Technology, Tai Nan, Taiwan
David McMurray	The International University of Kagoshima, Kagoshima, Japan
Mark Zeid	Hiroshima Gaigo Senmon Gakko, Hiroshima, Japan
Jean-Louis van der Merwe	KoJen ELS, Taipei, Taiwan
Michael Stout	Universal Language Institute, Tokyo, Japan
Peter Warner	At Home English, Nagoya, Japan
Sarah Tsai-Feng Yin	Caves Educational Training Co Ltd, Taipei, Taiwan
Cory Mcgowan	Yamasa English School, Okazaki, Japan
Gregory Mihaich	New Tokyo School, Kagoshima, Japan
Teachers from:	Shane English Schools, Japan; Lang Education Center, Hiroshima, Japan; Four Seasons Language School and Cultural Center, Hamamatsu, Japan

Table of Contents

Strategies	Situation	Collocation Sets
I wish I could find a way to ... I can't help the way I ... I don't like the way I ...	Giving advice	Attitude Thinking Prejudice
It's not as simple as that It's not as difficult as that You're missing the point	Buying and selling	Money Profit Price
It doesn't work like that ... just doesn't work. That might work	Questioning advice	Health Treatment Side effect
It's all because ... It all comes down to ... All ... have/has to do is ...	Helping a student	Exam Student Teacher
But that's not my main point That's beside the point ... getting away from the point	Deciding punishments	Crime Police Court
That's not realistic That's not practical You're exaggerating	Changing government policy	Environment Natural View
That's what I think, too That's where you're wrong That's what I was trying to say	An alien with problems	Space Solar Mystery
It's not just me who says this That's a very sweeping statement It's the other way around	To fight or not to fight	History Period War
at least/at most at first/at last The best/worst that can happen is ...	Boasting	Opportunity Sexual Man
What ... saying is ... ... not saying ... That's easy to say	Planning a factory	Aid Poverty Charity
... a nice argument, but ... ... tells me a lot about ... ... says more about ...	Making excuses	Violence Hit Fight
What would happen if ... ? What if ... ? How about if ... ?	Political manifestos	Election Vote Policy
In the long run ... The long-term effect ... The immediate effect ...	Starting a business	Economy Business Tax
... for a while, but ... ... for the time being, but ... ... n't last (very) long, but ...	Complaining	Happy Mood Satisfied
I wonder if it's as straightforward as ... It goes deeper than that I wonder if it's as clear cut as that	Giving a guided tour	International World Global

Characters

Tomoko
Japan

Jin-Sook
Korea

Chen
China

Annan
Thailand

Carlos
Brazil

Abena
Ghana

Francesca
Italy

Manosh
India

Christina
Sweden

Nazim
Turkey

1. Attitudes

WARM-UP QUESTIONS

Do you tend to trust new people you meet? For example?
Do you often feel people are against you? If so, when?
Do you like to be the center of attention? If so, when?
Could you marry somebody from a very different social background? Why?

VOCABULARY

Here are some words and expressions that will be useful in this unit.
How many do you know?

optimistic	prejudice	negative
tolerant	decisive	psychiatrist
broad-minded	pessimistic	narrow-minded
positive	easygoing	paranoid

Discuss which of the above words and expressions could fit in the following gaps.

Francesca: Maybe I'm ____. Whenever I'm in a serious relationship, I always think my boyfriend is playing around with other girls. I have these deep emotional fears, even if I know he's at home reading a book! I'd probably better see a ____.

Chen: That's surprising. You always seem so ____ and ____, so I've always imagined that you trust people without hesitation.

Francesca: Yes, everybody seems to see me as a ____ person who is always smiling and in a good mood, but in reality I'm about as ____ as they come, and I can't tolerate any of my boyfriend's flirting – real or imagined!

What words and expressions that are not in the list can you think of that might be useful when talking about attitudes?

MIND MAP

Here is Francesca's mind map starting from 'my character'.

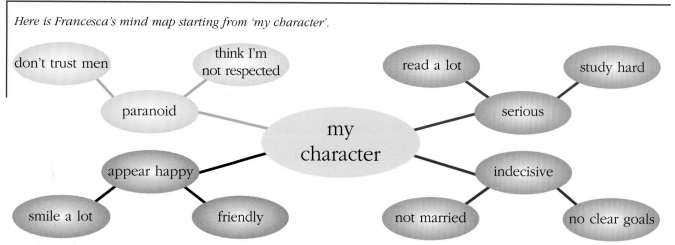

Now make your own mind maps with 'my character', 'my prejudices', 'my attitude to school/work', or 'my attitudes to people around me' in the center. Talk about your mind maps with another student or the rest of the class.

Made in America - Warner Bros, ph: Zade Rosenthal

POINTS OF VIEW - I COULD NEVER MARRY A FOREIGNER

I have a foreign boyfriend at the moment, but I could never get married to him. He would never completely understand me, and I'm sure we'd have arguments all the time. I wish I could find a way to be with him, but it seems impossible.

That's too pessimistic! And the sad thing is it will probably come true, but only because you believe it will. If you can find a way to be more optimistic, and stop thinking you'll have problems, you probably won't have them. If both of you go into your marriage with a positive attitude, you'll probably be very happy.

That may be true, but I can't help the way I feel. I do think we'd have arguments, and I can't change that, so I think it'd be better if I marry somebody who's more similar to me and who I can communicate with better. It would be much safer, and it would make my parents much happier, too.

I'm sorry to say this, but I think you're being negative and narrow-minded! Of course you can change the way you feel if you really want to. I think you need to take a close look at the reasons for your attitudes, and maybe move somewhere with your boyfriend where you can experience a more international environment.

Unit 1: Attitudes • 9

1. Attitudes

Practice and Discussion

PERSONALIZATION

Complete these sentences with your own ideas.

If I married … I'm sure we'd have arguments about …
I'm pessimistic about …
… will probably come true.
I have a positive attitude …
It may be true that …
I can … if I really want to.
I need to take a close look at …
I think I need to experience …

I need to take a close look at my attitude to work.

"Are you decisive?"
"Yes and no."

DISCUSSION

I don't like the way my boss talks to me.

DISCUSSION STRATEGIES

I wish I could find a way to …
I can't help the way I …
I don't like the way …

Try to include the discussion strategies and the patterns from the personalization section in the following discussions.

Does what we believe will happen often come true? For example?
Do you tend to be optimistic or pessimistic? For example?
What advice would you give somebody considering an international marriage?
What is the general attitude to international marriages in your country?
Do you think Tomoko's opinion is narrow-minded or sensible?
In which ways do you think you could develop and improve your attitudes?
What new experiences would you like to have?

Activities

FOLLOW-UP QUESTIONS

List three good points about your character and three bad points.

Example: I'm very optimistic.

Now talk to another student and ask at least two follow-up questions about each point.

Examples:

A: In what kinds of situations are you optimistic?

B: Almost always. I always believe I'll do well on a test, meet a new friend at a party, win a lottery …

A: Don't you feel disappointed when it doesn't happen?

B: No, I just believe something good will happen the next day.

ROLE PLAY

Student A: *TV reporter. Interview Student B about his attitudes to life.*

Student B: *Play the role of a famous person.*

Example questions:

How would you react if you lost your job?

How would you feel if your daughter wanted to marry somebody who … ?

What are the most important goals in your life?

SITUATION - GIVING ADVICE

Brainstorming: *Think of problems that cause stress.*
Think of good advice for each of these problems.
Think of reasons why it's difficult to follow each of the above pieces of advice.

Student A: *You are a psychiatrist. Try to advise Student B.*

Examples:

How long have you been feeling like this?

How often does that happen?

Have you tried not meeting him?

Student B: *You are a patient lying on the psychiatrist's couch. Choose one of these problems. Listen to Student A's advice and reject it with reasons.*

1. You are very lonely. 2. You don't like your job/school. 3. You always have arguments with people.
4. You are madly in love with a man/woman thirty years older than you. 5. You are afraid of butterflies.
6. You are a vampire.

Examples:

I've tried everything I can think of. I've even …
I don't know what to do! I can't live without her!
Every time I see a butterfly, I scream.

Now change roles, with Student B choosing a different problem.

"Doctor! Doctor! Everybody ignores me!"
"Next!"

1. Attitudes

Further Activities

COLLOCATION SETS

Put the following into sentences or dialogues.

Attitude

1. a friendly attitude   *Example:*   The person who interviewed me for the job had a very friendly attitude.
2. a responsible attitude
3. a patronizing attitude

Thinking

1. a way of thinking   *Example:*   We'll just have to accept that our ways of thinking are very different.
2. lateral thinking
3. quick thinking

Prejudice

1. racial prejudice   *Example:*   I came across so much racial prejudice when I first started working here.
2. overcome prejudice
3. deep-rooted prejudice

SPEECHES

Prepare a short speech on one of these three topics.

Genetics are the main factor in determining a person's character.
It is impossible to change our fundamental attitudes.
We should always be optimistic.

EXTRA EXPRESSIONS

Put the following into short dialogues.

coming or going   get on … nerves
couldn't care less   look on the bright side

Example:
A: You might get fired if you talk to him like that.
B: I couldn't care less!

"What a surprise meeting you here!"
"Are you coming or going?"
"I don't know. That's why I'm here."

Consolidation & Recycling

BUILDING VOCABULARY

Across

1   Female managers need to ___ a lot of prejudice.
4   ___ would be much safer.
6   I couldn't ___ less.
8   I hope I'll do well on the ___.
10   Find it difficult to make decisions.
11   I'd like to ___ and improve myself.
13   She's always happy and ___.
15   It may be true ___ I'm prejudiced.
17   You should ___ ___ your marriage positively.
22   It's best to live in an international ___.
23   A deep emotional ___.
24   Let's look on the bright ___.
25   The ___ thing is it may become true.

Down

1   Tend to be positive.
2   Relaxed about life.
3   Her parents may change their ___.
5   We'd fight all the ___.
7   Look up to.
9   I ___ to trust people.
12   The doctor is examining a ___.
14   I wonder if we'll ___ married.
16   I don't care what ___ to me.
18   He's playing around with ___ girls.
19   She gets on my ___.
20   I'll take a ___ look at the reasons.
21   I ___ people are against me.

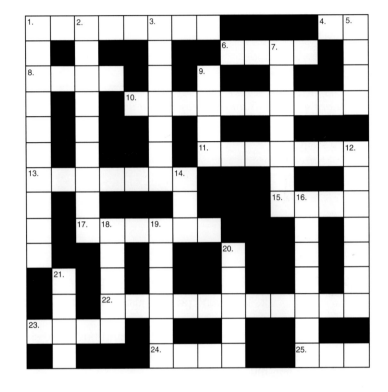

FOCUSING ON COLLOCATIONS

Write eight separate sentences, each of which includes both words in the pairs below.

friendly / attitude
center / attention
bright / side
play / around

racial / prejudice
way / thinking
without / hesitation
social / background

WRITING OPINIONS

Write paragraphs about the following. Try to include words and patterns from this unit.

What I'm worried about.
My prejudices.
The attitudes I'd like to have in future.

REFLECTION

Which section of the unit did you find most interesting?
In which section of the unit did you learn the most?
Make a list of any new words and patterns from this unit that you want to try and remember.
You may find it helpful to write each word or pattern on a card.

2. Money

WARM-UP QUESTIONS

Would you like to have a lot of money? Why?
If you had a lot of money, what would you do with it?
Would you change if you suddenly received a lot of money? If so, how?
Do you think you (will) work primarily for money? Why?

VOCABULARY

*Here are some words and expressions that will be useful in this unit.
How many do you know?*

greedy	interest	profit
incentive	earn	invest
deposit	stock market	amount
capital	value	loss

Discuss which of the above words and expressions could fit in the following gaps.

Christina: I have some money that I'd like to ____, but I'm not sure what to do with it. There's no point in just leaving it in the bank. It wouldn't ____ much ____.

Manosh: You could study the ____ and buy some shares in a company that's doing well, but it can be risky. There's no guarantee that the ____ of the shares will increase, so you run the risk of losing much of your money.

Christina: Yes, I might make a ____. Perhaps the safest way is to buy a new house or start my own small business. I could use my savings for the initial ____ for the house or as starting ____ for the business.

What words and expressions that are not in the list can you think of that might be useful when talking about money?

MIND MAP

Here is Christina's mind map starting from 'what to do with money'.

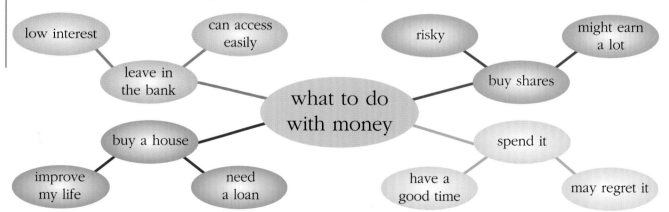

Now make your own mind map with 'what to do with money', 'the importance of money', 'a world without money', or 'how to get money' in the center. Talk about your mind map with another student or the rest of the class.

The Bourne Identity - Hypnotic/Universal, ph: Egon Endrenyi

POINTS OF VIEW - MONEY MAKES US GREEDY

Money is the main cause of selfishness and stress in human relationships. It makes us greedy and competitive. I think we should all get paid the same amount of money. Each of us could then choose what to do with that amount. Some of us would spend it on vacations, some of us on our homes ...

It's not as simple as that. How about people who don't want to work? Should they receive the same amount? Money is an incentive to work. If everybody received the same amount, many people wouldn't work hard. And we need competition to encourage us to continually develop and improve society. It's human nature.

Money is not the only incentive to work. Some people work hard because they like the people they are working with, or because they believe in the social value of what they are doing, or even just out of a sense of responsibility. When we focus on money, we tend to forget about these other incentives, and the quality of our lives suffers.

I wish you were right! But you're missing the point. Humans are basically greedy. It's not money that makes us greedy. We are greedy so we want money.

2. Money

Practice and Discussion

PERSONALIZATION

Complete these sentences with your own ideas.

> I think … causes stress in human relationships.
> I think … an incentive to work.
> If everybody received the same amount of money …
> I need/don't need competition to …
> I … out of a sense of responsibility.
> When I focus on …
> I tend to forget …
> My quality of life suffers when …

> *I tend to forget how lucky I am to have such a good job.*

"Why's that banker so unhappy?"
"He's lost interest in everything."

DISCUSSION

> *It's not as difficult as that. You just have to tell him frankly.*

DISCUSSION STRATEGIES

It's not as simple as that.
It's not as difficult/complicated as that.
You're missing the point.

Try to include the discussion strategies and the patterns from the personalization section in the following discussions.

Do you think money makes us selfish and greedy? Why?
Could you survive with only a little money? If so, how? If not, why not?
What are the best incentives to work?
What do you think are the best ways to save or invest money?
Is competition necessary?
Who should get the most money? Put the following jobs in the order in which you think they should get paid, and give reasons: a doctor, a refuse worker, a bank manager, a truck driver.

Activities

FOLLOW-UP QUESTIONS

List three reasons why people steal money.

Example: Because they are hungry.

Now talk to another student and ask at least two follow-up questions about each point.

Examples:

A: Why do they have to steal if they are hungry?

B: Because they can't get food or pay the rent any other way.

A: Why don't they get jobs and earn money to buy food?

B: Maybe there aren't enough jobs.

ROLE PLAY

Student A: *You are planning to start your own business.*

Student B: *Give Student A advice.*

Example questions:

What kind of business are you planning to have?
Where will you get some capital? How will you
   make a profit?

SITUATION - BUYING AND SELLING

Brainstorming: *Think of things you own that you might be prepared to sell.*
Think of ways of describing these things to impress potential buyers.
Think of ways to get money back for things you have bought.

Ist stage: *In groups, each of you starts with $1,000,000. Auction things you own to others in the group.*

Examples:

How much will you give me for my CD player?
It's in very good condition. I've only had it for one year.
It's worth much more than that. Won't somebody make
   me a better offer?

2nd stage: *After a time limit, each of you complains about the things you have bought and tries to sell them back.*

Examples:

You said it was as good as new, but it's covered in
   scratches.
If I'd known it was plastic, I wouldn't have offered so
   much.
You should have asked me what it was made of.

3rd stage: *After another time limit, make a list of what you own and how much money you have left.*

"What's the best way to become a millionaire?"
"Start with two million."

2. Money

Further Activities

COLLOCATION SETS

Put the following into sentences or dialogues.

Money
1. worth a lot of money   *Example:*   I think the antique watch my grandmother gave me is worth a lot of money.

2. a waste of money
3. raise money

Profit
1. gross profit   *Example:*   After we deduct taxes, the net profit will be a lot less than the gross profit.

2. make a profit
3. profit margin

Price
1. full price   *Example:*   Adults pay full price, and children are half price.
2. price range
3. a small price to pay

SPEECHES

Prepare a short speech on one of these three topics.

If people without much money work hard, they can become rich.
If we all had less money, we'd be much happier.
There should be a single currency for the whole world.

EXTRA EXPRESSIONS

Put the following into short dialogues.

earn a living   save for a rainy day
in debt   money doesn't grow on trees

Example:
A: It's very hard to earn a living these days.
B: Yes, I know. I think most people are finding things tough.

"Money doesn't grow on trees!"
"So why do banks have so many branches?"

Consolidation & Recycling

BUILDING VOCABULARY

Across

1   I'm trying to ___ money for charity.
4   A fight with words.
7   ___ should all get the same money.
9   My father has a very ___ attitude toward me.
11 I like to be the ___ of attention.
12 We'll need a ___ to buy that house.
13 The price ___ we can afford is not very high.
14 You'd ___ see a doctor.
16 You are ___ pessimistic!
17 There's no ___ in leaving it in the bank.
19 It's difficult to earn a ___.
21 It would make ___ parents happier.
22 I worry ___ when I know he's OK.
23 Pay no attention to somebody.
24 It doesn't work. It's a ___ of money.

Down

1   They work hard out of a sense of ___.
2   I even need to borrow for the ___ deposit.
3   We need competition to ___ us to work.
4   I don't know what to do. Please give me some ___.
5   The profit ___ is very low, so we can't give discounts.
6   I want to buy a ___ house.
8   ___ seems to see me as an optimist.
10 Money is an ___ to work.
15 Most people are finding ___ tough.
18 Money doesn't grow on ___.
20 I'm in a ___ mood today.

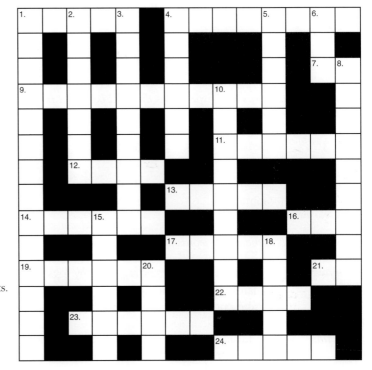

FOCUSING ON COLLOCATIONS

Write eight separate sentences, each of which includes both words in the pairs below.

make / profit
worth / money
serious / relationship
make / greedy

international / environment
full / price
earn / living
responsible / attitude

WRITING OPINIONS

Write paragraphs about the following. Try to include words and patterns from this unit.

The importance of money to me.
How to become rich.
Are humans basically greedy?

REFLECTION

Which section of the unit did you find most interesting?
In which section of the unit did you learn the most?
Make a list of any new words and patterns from this unit that you want to try and remember.
You may find it helpful to write each word or pattern on a card.

3. Health

WARM-UP QUESTIONS

How do you take care of your health?
Do you avoid some kinds of food? Which foods? Why?
How much exercise do you get?
How would you like to take better care of your health in the future?

VOCABULARY

Here are some words and expressions that will be useful in this unit.
How many do you know?

medicine	aches	side effects
sore	rash	insurance
prescribe	injury	swollen
ointments	treatment	stiff

Discuss which of the above words and expressions could fit in the following gaps.

Tomoko: I played tennis yesterday, and my legs are very _swo_ and _stiff_ today. I can hardly walk. It's not a sports ____ or anything like that. I just usually don't take enough exercise, so my body ____ all over.

Nazim: I know how you feel. Exercise can sometimes do more harm than good! But, don't worry! I have some great ____ that will clear everything up in no time. You just rub it into your ____ muscles a couple of times a day.

Tomoko: Thank you for the offer, but I think I'll see a doctor. I have a lot of allergies, and if I'm not careful I could easily get a ____ all over my legs. It's incredible how even very common creams and ____ can have serious ____.

What words and expressions that are not in the list can you think of that might be useful when talking about health?

MIND MAP

Here is Tomoko's mind map starting from 'allergies'.

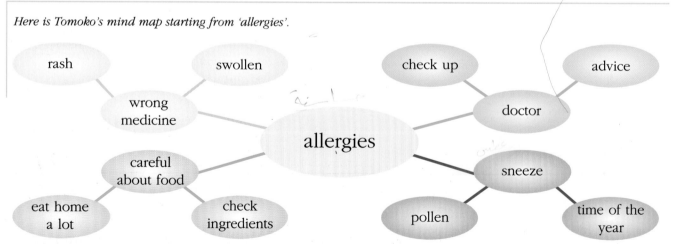

Now make your own mind map with 'allergies', 'keeping healthy', 'doctors', or 'paying for health' in the center.
Talk about your mind map with another student or the rest of the class.

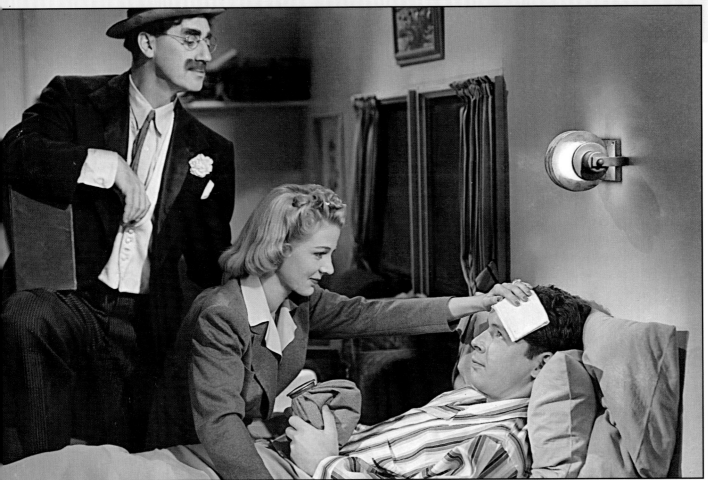

At the Circus - MGM

POINTS OF VIEW - MEDICAL CARE SHOULD BE FREE

I think medical care should be free for everybody. Health care is a basic human right, so the rich shouldn't get better medical care than the poor. This is only possible if all doctors and nurses are employed by the government, and all treatment is given according to need. Money should play no part in deciding who gets treatment and who doesn't.

Speak play back

That wouldn't work in practice. When doctors are civil servants, they don't care so much about their patients. When they have their own hospitals or surgeries, they care much more – if they don't give good treatment, they lose patients. Market forces can be very effective in keeping doctors on their toes.

It doesn't work like that. Private doctors often prescribe medicine for patients who are not really sick. They make more money that way. It's also what many of their patients want. If a doctor refuses to give unnecessary treatment, the patients will just go to another doctor. So when market forces are applied to health care, it leads to waste, and poorer patients who really need help have to wait longer for treatment.

It's true that private medical systems have problems, but government health care just doesn't work! When medical care is provided by the government, young people have to pay too much tax to support old people. This reduces incentives, makes the economy less dynamic, and then the government can't afford to provide free health care any more.

3. Health

Practice and Discussion

PERSONALIZATION

Complete these sentences with your own ideas.

how

Health care is a basic human right.
... should play no part in ...health care...
Market forces can be very effective in keeping doctors on
their toes.
... keep(s) me on my toes.
I refuse to ...
Market forces can't be applied to ...
... reduce(s) my incentive to work/study.
I can't afford to ...

I can't afford
to go abroad
very often.

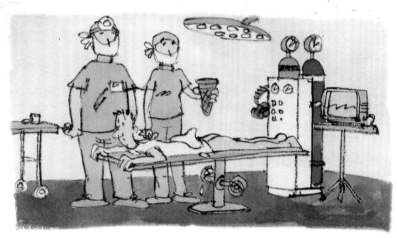

"That operation sent a shiver down my spine."
"So that's what happened to my ice cream."

DISCUSSION

I could tell my boyfriend
I had to work late, but I
know it wouldn't work.

DISCUSSION STRATEGIES

It doesn't work like that.
It/they just doesn't/don't work!
It/that might/could/wouldn't work.

Try to include the discussion strategies and the patterns from the personalization section in the following discussions.

Do you think it is OK for the rich to get better medical care than the poor? Why?
What are the positive and negative effects of market forces on health care?
Describe the health care system in your country. How can it be improved?
Do you think doctors deserve large salaries?
Should doctors be civil servants?
Do you think health is a basic human right so medical treatment should be free? Why?
What things are basic human rights?

Activities

FOLLOW-UP QUESTIONS

List three qualities you think a good doctor should have.

Example: A doctor should care about all patients
(مساواة) equally.

Now talk to another student and ask at least two follow-up questions about each point.

Examples:
A: Why is it so important for doctors to treat patients equally?
B: It's their professional responsibility.
A: What would happen if they didn't?
B: Some patients might become very sick or die unnecessarily.

ROLE PLAY

Student A: *You are a doctor. Give Student B advice and prescribe treatment.*
Student B: *You are a patient with a problem (some possible problems: you have a broken leg, a stiff neck, a backache, an allergy to work/ school, you always feel tired, you are overweight).*

Example questions:
What exactly is the problem?
Does it hurt when I do this?
How long have you been feeling like this?

SITUATION - QUESTIONING ADVICE

Brainstorming: *Think of advice patterns.*
Think of problems a superstar might go to see a doctor for.
Think of ways to question advice.

Student A: *You are a doctor. Give Student B advice.*
Student B: *You are a superstar (choose the person) with a problem. Question Student A's advice.*

Example problems:
I'm losing my voice, and I have a concert tomorrow
   night.
I've twisted my ankle, and there's a big soccer game on
   Saturday.
I have hiccups, and I have to read the news on TV
   tonight.
I'm allergic to cows, and I'm starring in a western.

Example questioning:
But if I gargle every hour, I'll wake up the neighbors.
I tried bandaging my ankle last time, but I couldn't turn
   quickly.
Don't you think that if somebody hits me on the back,
   all the TV viewers will be surprised?
It's a good idea to use plastic cows, but I don't think
   the Director would agree.

Take turns to be the famous person with a problem.

"Doctor! Doctor! I only have 59 seconds left to live!"
"Sit down over there. I'll see you in a minute."

3. Health

Further Activities

COLLOCATION SETS

Put the following into sentences or dialogues.

Health

1. neglect ... health

2. good for ... health
3. take care of ... health

Example: He eats all the wrong kinds of food, never takes any exercise, and neglects his health in so many other ways.

Treatment

1. respond to treatment
2. receive treatment
3. emergency treatment

Example: I think he's going to recover. He's responding to treatment.

Side effect

1. a harmful side effect

2. an unexpected side effect
3. suffer from a side effect

Example: You can take these tablets three times a day. There are no harmful side effects.

SPEECHES

Prepare a short speech on one of these three topics.

A healthy body leads to a healthy mind.
Aids is the result of a decline in our morality.
We should pay more attention to alternative medicine.

EXTRA EXPRESSIONS

Put the following into short dialogues.

go in one ear and out the
   other
a slip of the tongue

give/lend ... a hand
There's more to it than
   meets the eye.

Example:
A: I'm never going to finish this work in time.
B: Shall I give you a hand?

"There's more to a grapefruit than meets the eye."

Consolidation & Recycling

BUILDING VOCABULARY

Across
1   Tend to think things will go badly.
7   It's ___ what many of their patients want.
8   I have deep ___ fears.
9   You should ___ thinking you'll have problems.
10 I can't walk. I have a broken ___.
13 How would you ___ if you lost your job?
14 I'd better ___ a doctor.
15 I wish I could ___ with her.
17 It was ___ ___ of the tongue.
18 Money is the ___ cause of selfishness.
19 He ___ a lot of money.
21 Money should ___ no part in it.
23 She interviewed me ___ the job.
26 I wish my back didn't ___ so much!
27 I always ___ you to be optimistic.
28 I pulled a ___ in my leg and it's very stiff.

Down
1   Some doctors ___ too much medicine.
2   Your arms look ___. They are not usually so big.
3   I'm in a very bad ___ today!
4   You'll get fired if you ___ to your boss like that.
5   What is the main ___ of stress?
6   Rub it in a ___ of times a day.
11 The ___ profit is the amount before taxes are deducted.
12 There's a lot of ___ prejudice in my office.
14 My leg's so ___! It's difficult to move.
16 It went in through one ___ and out the other.
17 I twisted my ___ while playing tennis.
20 The opposite of 'loss'.
21 The amount we must pay.
22 Give me ___ ___. This is too heavy!
24 It can do more ___ than good.
25 Rub it ___ your legs.

FOCUSING ON COLLOCATIONS

Write eight separate sentences, each of which includes both words in the pairs below.

receive / treatment   human / right
social / value   harmful / side
patronizing / attitude   civil / servant
overcome / prejudice   slip / tongue

WRITING OPINIONS

Write paragraphs about the following. Try to include words and patterns from this unit.

Keeping healthy.
Doctors.
A sickness I once had.

REFLECTION

Which section of the unit did you find most interesting?
In which section of the unit did you learn the most?
Make a list of any new words and patterns from this unit that you want to try and remember.
You may find it helpful to write each word or pattern on a card.

4. Education

WARM-UP QUESTIONS

What are/were your favorite school subjects? Why?

What was/has been your favorite year at school? Why?

What things make/made you study hard?

What changes would you like to see in schools?

VOCABULARY

Here are some words and expressions that will be useful in this unit. How many do you know?

rules	memorize	motivation
graduate	co-education	student-centered
syllabus	curriculum	compulsory
bullying	subjects	single sex

Discuss which of the above words and expressions could fit in the following gaps.

Carlos: I only went to ____ schools. There were no girls at all. It was so unnatural! And the style of teaching was so old-fashioned! The ____ wasn't flexible at all. All ____ were ____ until we were seventeen, and then we could make a few choices.

Annan: I bet you studied many ____ that I'll never get a chance to know much about. At the schools I went to, we had a lot of freedom of choice, but I often wonder if we learned enough. One very good thing was that lessons tended to be ____, so most of us were motivated to study at home by ourselves.

Carlos: That's great! Your teachers obviously understood the importance of self- ____. We just followed ____ and did what we were told. There was nothing to entice us to study for ourselves. And the strictness and hierarchy led to a lot of ____ as well.

What words and expressions that are not in the list can you think of that might be useful when talking about education?

MIND MAP

Here is Carlos' mind map starting from 'my school'.

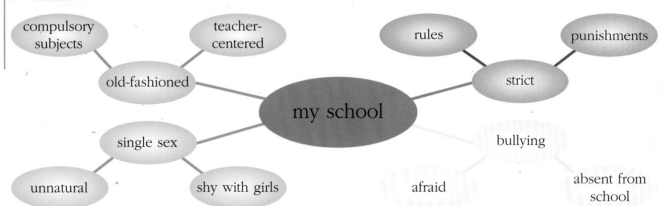

Now make your own mind map with 'my school', 'a good teacher', 'school subjects', or 'school rules' in the center. Talk about your mind map with another student or the rest of the class.

POINTS OF VIEW - TEACHERS SHOULD LET STUDENTS LEARN

Why do teachers like to talk so much? I'm fed up with listening to them. I want to find things out for myself, but most of my teachers never give me a chance. Even when they do, it's only for a short time. All they have to do is stop explaining, stop telling me what to do, and let me think things through for myself. I'd learn a lot more that way.

It's all because of the syllabus. If we are given a lot of time to discover things for ourselves, the teacher would never get through the syllabus. So we have to just memorize a lot of facts for exams, and when we're older we'll have more time to choose the things we want to learn.

By that time I probably won't be so interested in learning new things. It'll all feel like studying. The school system just destroys our curiosity and creativity. After studying at school for a few years, the only things most of us are really interested in have nothing to do with school, like music, bikes, or sport. It's all because of the way we are taught.

Well, I think the system works well. I love mathematics, and after I graduate I'm going to become a mathematics teacher, and I'll teach in exactly the same way we have been taught. It's worked for me, so it should work for everybody else.

4. Education

Practice and Discussion

PERSONALIZATION

Complete these sentences with your own ideas.

I want to find out … for myself.
… never give me a chance to …
I need to think things through when …
If I had a lot of time to … I'd …
By the time I'm … I … any more.
… nothing to do with …
I … in exactly the same way as …
… works/has worked for me.

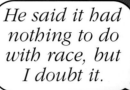

He said it had nothing to do with race, but I doubt it.

"One of the students has just swallowed his pencil. What should I do?"
"Let him use a pen."

DISCUSSION

At the end of the day, it all comes down to money.

DISCUSSION STRATEGIES

It's all because …
It all comes down to …
All … have/has to do is …

Try to include the discussion strategies and the patterns from the personalization section in the following discussions.

Why do some teachers talk so much?
In what ways can teachers encourage students to think things through more?
How important is it to memorize facts?
Do you agree that the school system tends to destroy curiosity and creativity?
Do you think the education system in your country works well?
How could the way of teaching English be improved?
Which of the students on page 27 do you agree with most? Why?

Activities

FOLLOW-UP QUESTIONS

List three qualities of a good teacher.

Example: A good teacher shouldn't have favorite students.

Now talk to another student and ask at least two follow-up questions about each point.

Examples:
A: Don't you think it's natural for a teacher to like some students better?
B: It's unprofessional and it can make other students feel insecure.
A: I think teachers should be humans, not robots.
B: Yes, sure. They should be as human as possible. But they should also be fair.

ROLE PLAY

Student A: *You are a teacher trying to help Student A.*
Student B: *You are a student wondering what to do after graduating (choose whether you are graduating from high school or college).*

Example questions:
What kind of life do you want to have ten years from now?
Have you considered studying to become a nurse?

SITUATION - HELPING A STUDENT

Brainstorming: *Think of reasons why a student might be absent from school.*
                     Think of rules a student might break.
                     Think of ways a teacher can help in each case.

Student A: *You are a teacher talking to a student who is often absent from school and breaks many school rules.*

Examples:
Why are you absent so often?
Don't you care if you fail your exams?
Has anybody been bullying you?

Student B: *You are the problem student.*

Examples:
I'm not interested in school any more.
I don't want to study medicine. I want to be an astronaut.
I don't care what happens to me in the future.

"I don't want to go to school! I'm so unpopular! The students bully me! The teachers don't like me! I want to stay home and play computer games."
"But Dad! You have to go! You're the Principal!"

Further Activities

COLLOCATION SETS

Put the following into sentences or dialogues.

Exam (examination)

1. pass an exam   *Example:*   She was sure she would fail the exam, but, in fact, she passed.
2. retake (resit) an exam
3. an oral exam

Student

1. a conscientious student   *Example:*   She's one of the most conscientious students in the class. She always does her homework and tries hard.
2. a student loan
3. a mature student

Teacher

1. a qualified teacher   *Example:*   We only employ qualified teachers with a professional attitude.
2. an experienced teacher
3. teacher-centered

SPEECHES

Prepare a short speech on one of these three topics.

School fees should vary according to the income of a student's parents.
There should be no school uniforms.
All schools should be co-educational.

EXTRA EXPRESSIONS

Put the following into short dialogues.

over ... head   with ... eyes closed
in a class of ... own   learn from experience

Example:
A: How was the lesson?
B: It was way over my head.

"You got '0' in your exam again! When I was your age, I could do tests like this with my eyes closed!"
"Yes, but you had a different teacher."

Consolidation & Recycling

BUILDING VOCABULARY

Across

1 Cares and tries hard.
6 ___ reality, I'm pessimistic.
7 If I spend all my money, I may ___ it.
9 Our teachers needs to get through the ___.
10 I tend to ___ new people I meet.
11 ___ this cream into your legs every day.
12 Not everybody ___ a housing loan.
13 There was nothing to ___ us to study.
15 We should all get paid the same ___.
17 He doesn't play ___ with other girls.
19 I'm careful about the ___ I eat.
20 I don't know whether I'm ___ or going.
21 The teacher's attitude ___ ___ a lot of bullying.
22 I couldn't accept her advice. I had to ___ it.

Down

1 The school ___ wasn't flexible at all.
2 I think you're being ___ and narrow-minded!
3 Educating boys and girls together.
4 Don't ___ me what to do!
5 In what kind of ___ are you optimistic?
8 It's out of the price ___ I can afford.
9 The ___ at school put pressure on everybody.
14 Make something better.
16 It's all because of the way we are ___ at school.
17 I ___ unhealthy food.
18 When I work too hard, the quality of my ___ suffers.

FOCUSING ON COLLOCATIONS

Write eight separate sentences, each of which includes both words in the pairs below.

qualified / teacher
conscientious / student
get / through
emergency / treatment

good / health
market / forces
student / loan
small / pay

WRITING OPINIONS

Write paragraphs about the following. Try to include words and patterns from this unit.

A teacher I respect.
School bullying.
How English could be taught more effectively.

REFLECTION

Which section of the unit did you find most interesting?
In which section of the unit did you learn the most?
Make a list of any new words and patterns from this unit that you want to try and remember.
You may find it helpful to write each word or pattern on a card.

5. Crime

WARM-UP QUESTIONS

If somebody stole $10,000 from you, what would you do?
What do you think should happen to the thief? Why?
Why do people commit serious crimes? Think of various possible reasons.
What should the government or police do to reduce crime?

VOCABULARY

Here are some words that will be useful in this unit.
How many do you know?

innocent	evidence	trial
court	arrested	motive
criminal	sentenced	suspicion
convicted	witness	suspected

Discuss which of the above words could fit in the following gaps.

Manosh: I was ____ once. I was ____, of course. I didn't do anything illegal, but a ____ identified me through a computer search, and I had no alibi, so I was ____ by the police. It was an absurd situation. I had no connection with the crime at all, and no ____ to commit it.

Jin-Sook: That must have been a terrible experience. Was there a ____? Did you have to appear in ____? Were you ____? I suppose everything turned out OK in the end. It must have done, or you wouldn't be here now.

Manosh: Fortunately, it never went to ____. If I'd been prosecuted and found guilty, I could have been ____ to a few years in prison. But I was branded as a ____ for a few months. Even some of my best friends began to doubt me, and I had to change jobs because of all the ____ around me at work.

What words and expressions that are not in the list can you think of that might be useful when talking about crime?

MIND MAP

Here is Manosh's mind map starting from 'arrested'.

Now make your own mind map with 'arrested', 'criminals', 'the death penalty', or 'the police' in the center.
Talk about your mind map with another student or the rest of the class.

Keystone Cops - Sennett Films

POINTS OF VIEW - THE DEATH PENALTY IS NECESSARY

Murderers and terrorists should be punished by death. If all murderers were executed, there'd be far less violent crime. And, anyway, if somebody deliberately takes another person's life, they have no right to live.

There's no evidence to show that the death penalty has any effect on the number of murders. In the United States, some states have the death penalty and some don't, but there is no noticeable difference in the murder rates. Most killers act in the heat of the moment, and they don't seem to consider the consequences of their actions.

That's beside the point. Why should we spend large amounts of money keeping murderers in prison for many years? And why should they be free to kill more innocent people after they are released? We have to protect society, and the only way to do this is by sentencing murderers and terrorists to death.

The whole process of sentencing somebody to death is also very expensive. But that's not my main point. A far more important consideration is that if a society has the death penalty, it is telling every member of that society that violence and killing are ways to deal with problems. It also says that human beings sometimes have the right to take other human beings' lives. Shouldn't society be setting a better example?

Unit 5: Crime • 33

5. Crime

Practice and Discussion

PERSONALIZATION

Complete these sentences with your own ideas.

If one person deliberately takes another person's life …
I have a right to …
There's no evidence to show that …
I sometimes … in the heat of the moment.
I sometimes don't consider the consequences when I …
One way to protect society is …
A good way to deal with criminals is …
I have to set a good example to …

I have a right to know who told you about my dinner with Manosh!

"Is there any difference between 'against the law' and 'illegal'?"
"Yes, of course. If something is against the law, we shouldn't do it.
And illegal is a sick bird."

DISCUSSION

You're getting away from the point. Did you pinch me or not?!

DISCUSSION STRATEGIES

But that's not my main point.
That's beside the point.
… getting away from the point.

Try to include the discussion strategies and the patterns from the personalization section in the following discussions.

Do you think the death penalty is justifiable for certain crimes? If so, which ones?
Why do you think we should send people to prison? to protect other people? out of revenge? to help criminals reform? or for another reason?
Would you ever break the law? Why? If so, when?
Are there any laws you disagree with? If so, which ones?
Do you trust and respect the police and the courts? Why?
What are the most important things a judge should consider when sentencing a criminal?

Activities

FOLLOW-UP QUESTIONS

List three reasons why a criminal's punishments should be less than it normally would be for the kind of crime he/she has committed.

Example: If the criminal has a family to support.

Now talk to another student and ask at least two follow-up questions about each point.

Examples:

A: Even criminals with families should obey the law.

B: Not necessarily, if they commit the crime to help their families, not themselves.

A: Shouldn't they just apply for welfare?

B: That's easy to say, but they may not think the government will help them very much.

ROLE PLAY

Student A: *You are a police officer. A gorilla has just escaped from the zoo. Question Student A.*

Student B: *You are a gorilla pretending to be a human. Give reasons for having the keys to the zoo, a plane ticket to Africa, driving a truck full of bananas, and having a very hairy body. (Bang your chest when you get excited).*

Example questions:
Where did you get those keys?
Why do you need so many bananas?
Did you forget to shave this morning?

SITUATION - DECIDING PUNISHMENTS

Brainstorming: *Think of possible crimes.*
Think of possible excuses for crimes.
Think of possible punishments.

Student A: *You have committed a crime (choose the crime). Explain why you committed the crime and why you should not be punished.*

Examples:
I took his money because he's very rich, and my family doesn't even have a place to live.
My car doesn't need brakes. I always drive slowly.
I killed him because I found he had another wife as well as me.

Student B: *You are a judge and must decide whether and how Student A should be punished. Ask questions and then decide the punishment.*

Examples:
Why did you hit him so hard?
Don't you think it's dangerous for other drivers?
I sentence you to three years in prison.

Student A and B take turns to be the criminal and the judge, choosing a different crime each time.

"You are accused of stealing underwear from this lady's washing line."
"Please don't punish me. It was my first slip."

5. Crime

Further Activities

COLLOCATION SETS

Put the following into sentences or dialogues.

Crime

1. crime rate   *Example:*   It doesn't matter what the government does, the crime rate continues to increase.

2. commit a crime
3. investigate a crime

Police

1. the police ... question   *Example:*   There was a murder in my neighborhood recently. The police have questioned many suspects, but I don't think they've caught the person who did it.

2. the police ... arrest
3. call the police

Court

1. court case   *Example:*   In a recent court case, a man was accused of poisoning his wife.
2. Supreme Court
3. settle out of court

SPEECHES

Prepare a short speech on one of these three topics.

If criminals go to prison, they feel rejected by society and are more likely to commit crimes again.

It is not a crime to steal from the rich to give to the poor.

Humans are naturally aggressive and need strict laws for their own protection.

EXTRA EXPRESSIONS

Put the following into short dialogues.

look into   get away with
jump to conclusions   it serves ... right

Example:
A: I've failed the exam!
B: It serves you right! You should have studied harder!

"A hole has been discovered in the fence around the nudist camp. The police are looking into it."

Consolidation & Recycling

BUILDING VOCABULARY

Across
1. His prejudices are too ___ to be removed.
6. It's not as simple as ___.
7. Those who take another person's ___ have no right to live.
8. It has no effect on the ___ of murders.
9. It will probably ___ true.
11. She ___ the school rules very conscientiously.
14. I couldn't prove I wasn't at the bank. I had no ___.
17. The curriculum wasn't flexible ___ all.
18. You are ___ of stealing a painting.
19. Our teachers don't have to ___ everything to us.
20. Why did you ___ him so hard?
21. There's no ___ to show that it has any effect.
22. It's worth a lot of ___.
23. The judge may ___ you to one year in prison.

Down
1. He ___ took her life.
2. This medicine has a harmful side ___.
3. She's self-employed. She has her ___ hospital.
4. It's only for a short ___.
5. I think you are negative and ___-minded!
6. If there's a ___, I'll be found innocent.
10. Our teachers understand the importance of self-___.
12. We should ___ a better example.
13. My teacher never gives me a ___ to learn for myself.
15. I need to ___ potential buyers in order to sell my house.
16. The highest court is the ___ Court.
17. I'm in trouble and need some good ___ from my friends.

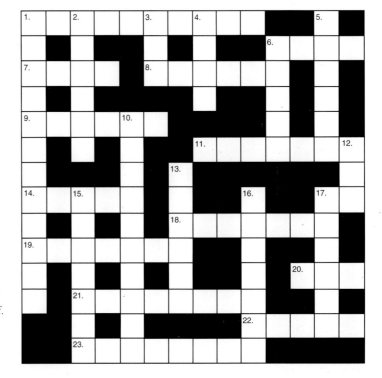

FOCUSING ON COLLOCATIONS

Write eight separate sentences, each of which includes both words in the pairs below.

call / police
learn / experience
allergic / to
profit / margin

death / penalty
investigate / crime
deep-rooted / prejudice
jump / conclusions

very strong

WRITING OPINIONS

Write paragraphs about the following. Try to include words and patterns from this unit.

The police.
The death penalty.
The purpose of prison.

REFLECTION

Which section of the unit did you find most interesting?
In which section of the unit did you learn the most?
Make a list of any new words and patterns from this unit that you want to try and remember.
You may find it helpful to write each word or pattern on a card.

6. The Environment

WARM-UP QUESTIONS

How is the world's climate changing?
What do you think the causes of these changes are?
Name five sources of pollution.
What can we do to improve the environment?

VOCABULARY

Here are some words and expressions that will be useful in this unit.
How many do you know?

rain forests	nuclear waste	emissions
ozone layer	ecosystem	global warming
pesticides	organic farming	toxic chemicals
acid rain	deforestation	greenhouse effect

Discuss which of the above words and expressions could fit in the following gaps.

Abena: The weather is completely different from what it was like twenty years ago.
           I'm sure it's all because of ____ caused by the ____. It's frightening.

Chen: So many of these problems are simply the side effects of industrialization, consumerism, and
           exploitation of poorer countries. It's probably too late to do anything. Even if we cut down on
           carbon dioxide ____ and replant the ____, it won't make much difference.

Abena: I hope you aren't right, but it does look like we may have permanently destroyed the Earth's ____ in
           so many ways. To stand any chance at all, we have to stop using ____ and ____, stop polluting the
           air and water, and radically change our way of life.

What words and expressions that are not in the list can you think of that might be useful when talking about the
environment?

MIND MAP

Here is Abena's mind map starting from 'what we can do'.

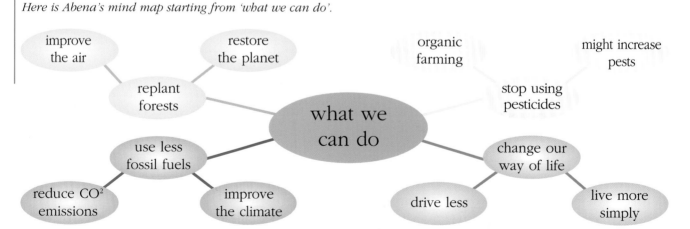

Now make your own mind map with 'what we can do', 'environmental problems', 'the changing climate', or 'organic
farming' in the center. Talk about your mind map with another student or the rest of the class.

Sound of Music - 20th Century Fox

POINTS OF VIEW - RICH COUNTRIES HAVE TO TAKE DRASTIC ACTION

I think everybody in the richer countries should pay an environment tax, and the income from this taxation should be paid to an international organization set up by the United Nations. This organization would be responsible for dealing with problems like the thinning of the ozone layer and deforestation.

That's not realistic. The economies of the developed countries aren't strong enough, and there are a lot of other things we have to spend our money on.

If we don't do something drastic, the polar ice caps will melt, many people will die of cancer caused by too much ultra-violet radiation, and the world's ecosystem will be permanently damaged. The human race may not survive much longer.

You're exaggerating! It's not as bad as all that. We just have to be more careful. All countries need to get together and agree on international policies for protecting the environment. This is beginning to happen now, and I'm sure more progress will be made in the near future.

6. The Environment

Practice and Discussion

PERSONALIZATION

Complete these sentences with your own ideas.

I think everybody in the richer countries should ...
The income from an increase in taxation should be spent on ...
The economies of the developing countries aren't strong
    enough to ...
If we don't do something drastic ...
I think the human race ...
All countries need to get together and ...
We all have to agree ...
I'm sure ... in the near future.

If I don't do something drastic, I'll never get married!

*"Do you know that an innocent animal suffered a lot of pain
so you could have that fur coat?"*
"Don't talk about my husband like that!"

DISCUSSION

You're exaggerating! Of course you can't go faster than me!

DISCUSSION STRATEGIES

That's not realistic.
That's not practical.
You're exaggerating!

Try to include the discussion strategies and the patterns from the personalization section in the following discussions.

How serious do you think the world's environmental problems are? Why?
Do you think all countries in the world will get together to solve these problems?
    Why?
Would people in richer countries pay more tax to help those in poorer countries?
Is your local environment improving or getting worse? Give examples.
What are the main things that can be done to improve the environment?
How can talk be transferred into action?
How long do you think the human race will survive?

Activities

FOLLOW-UP QUESTIONS

List three ways in which the natural environment is changing.

Example: The rain forests are being cut down.

Now talk to another student and ask at least two follow-up questions about each point.

Examples:

A: What will happen if more rain forests are destroyed?

B: There won't be enough oxygen in the atmosphere.

A: Why is that so important?

B: All living things need oxygen in order to survive.

ROLE PLAY

Student A: You think it's best to only eat organically grown food.

Student B: You like to eat anything that tastes good. Argue with Student A.

Example opinions:
Vegetables sprayed with pesticides may cause cancer.
It's more fun to eat anything we like. We should enjoy our lives!

SITUATION - CHANGING GOVERNMENT POLICY

Brainstorming: *Think of ways to improve the environment.*
Think of why it may be difficult to make each of these changes.
Think of how governments could find money to make these changes.

Student A: *You are an environmental activist trying to persuade the President/Prime Minister to support an environment tax, close down all nuclear power plants, ban hunting, ban all cars which emit too much carbon dioxide, etc.*

Examples:
It takes generations for nuclear waste to become safe.
Many people have died, but the government keeps it secret.
The future of the world is at stake.

Student B: *You are the President/Prime Minister. You want to avoid doing any of the things Student A wants you to do.*

Examples:
We're doing our best to deal with the disposal of nuclear waste, but it takes time.
That's not practical. Where would the money come from?
If we banned those cars, the buses and trains would be too crowded.

"What do you put on your strawberries?"
"Only natural manure!"
"That's unusual. I put cream on mine."

6. The Environment

Further Activities

COLLOCATION SETS

Put the following into sentences or dialogues.

Environment

1. protect the environment   *Example:*   Much more needs to be done to protect the environment from toxic chemicals.

2. harm the environment
3. adapt to the environment

Natural

1. natural habitat   *Example:*   I was surprised to see the ducks on the lake near my house. They are so far away from their natural habitat.

2. natural ingredients
3. look natural

View

1. spoil the view   *Example:*   Pylons may be necessary, but they often spoil the view.
2. a breathtaking view
3. block the view

SPEECHES

Prepare a short speech on one of these three topics.

It's too late to save the Earth. It's time to look for another planet to live on.
The cause of all our environmental problems is greed.
Environmentalists exaggerate problems like pollution.

EXTRA EXPRESSIONS

Put the following into short dialogues.

make a mountain out of a
    molehill
can't see the forest for the
    trees

it wasn't ... fault
the tip of the iceberg

Example:
A: I heard that one of your players failed a drug test.
B: I'm afraid it's just the tip of the iceberg.
    There are many more players who take drugs and get away with it.

"That was a big tremor!"
"It wasn't my fault."

Consolidation & Recycling

BUILDING VOCABULARY

Across

2   Your teachers ___ understood the importance of self motivation.
6   ___ warming.
8   Pollution will ___ the ecosystem.
10 That will ___ you right!
11 Treatment is given according to ___.
13 ___ forests.
14 We have to memorize a lot of facts for the ___.
17 In a recent court ___, a man was accused of murdering his wife.
19 We need to change our way of ___.
21 My body hurts ___ over.
22 Yes ___ no.
23 She usually ___ new people she meets.
24 I was ___ as a criminal.
26 I was fired and had to look for a new ___.
28 Take this ___ three times a day.

Down

1   ___ farming.
2   The ___ layer.
3   Against the law.
4   Look on the bright ___.
5   The ___ effect.
7   I'm about as pessimistic ___ they come.
9   Animals need to ___ to a new environment.
12 I have ___ emotional fears.
15 A healthy body leads to a healthy ___.
16 We must stop spraying vegetables with ___.
18 I'm ___ to pollen.
20 What was your favorite ___ at school?
25 It sent a shiver ___ my spine.
27 We'll need to borrow some money from the ___.
28 He would never understand ___.

FOCUSING ON COLLOCATIONS

Write eight separate sentences, each of which includes both words in the pairs below.

block / view
commit / crime
oral / exam
tip / iceberg

nuclear / waste
look / natural
neglect / health
something / drastic

WRITING OPINIONS

Write paragraphs about the following. Try to include words and patterns from this unit.

Global warming.
Organic farming.
What each of us can do to improve the environment.

REFLECTION

Which section of the unit did you find most interesting?
In which section of the unit did you learn the most?
Make a list of any new words and patterns from this unit that you want to try and remember.
You may find it helpful to write each word or pattern on a card.

7. Aliens

WARM-UP QUESTIONS

Do you think there is intelligent life on other planets? Why?
Do you think aliens have visited the Earth in UFOs? Why?
If UFOs exist, do you think they are friendly or dangerous? Why?
Do you think aliens could be living among us? Why?

VOCABULARY

Here are some words and expressions that will be useful in this unit.
How many do you know?

UFOs	universe	science fiction
dimension	speed of light	astronomers
solar system	flying saucers	sightings
black holes	outer space	galaxies

Discuss which of the above words and expressions could fit in the following gaps.

Nazim: I wonder if people will ever be able to travel to other ____. Rockets will need to travel faster than the ____, ____ will have to identify planets that can support human life, and there'll be many other problems to overcome. I wonder if it will ever happen.

Annan: There have been many ____ of ____ that seem to have come from ____. So, if aliens can visit us, I expect we'll be able to visit their planets one day.

Nazim: I know it must sound like I read too much ____, but maybe we'll discover some completely new technology that enables us to travel through ____ or shift into another ____ so as to cover distances much faster.

What words and expressions that are not in the list can you think of that might be useful when talking about aliens?

MIND MAP

Here is Nazim's mind map starting from 'space travel'.

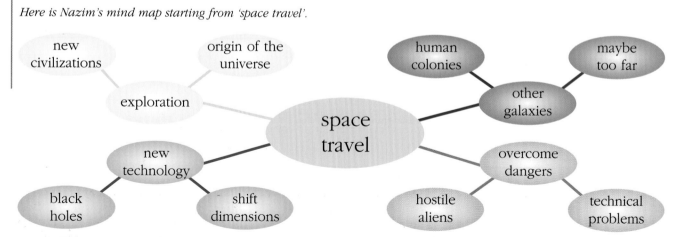

Now make your own mind map with 'space travel', 'UFOs', 'life on other planets', or 'new technologies' in the center.
Talk about your mind map with another student or the rest of the class.

Independence Day - 20th Century Fox

POINTS OF VIEW - THERE IS INTELLIGENT LIFE ON OTHER PLANETS

There must be intelligent life on other planets. The universe is so large, and the Earth is just one small insignificant planet. It's very arrogant to assume we are the only intelligent beings.

Astronomers have been looking for signs of intelligent life on other planets for years but have never found anything. Anyway, if there are intelligent aliens, some of them should have visited us by now. We're in a young part of the universe, so some aliens in older parts of the universe should have much more advanced technology than ours, and some of them should be able to travel to the Earth by now.

That's what I think, too. And I'm sure they've already visited us. That's why there are so many reported sightings of UFOs. I think some governments know there is intelligent life on other planets, and probably even have evidence of UFOs, but keep their knowledge secret. They probably think we're not ready to know what's really going on.

That's where you're wrong. That wouldn't happen in a democratic society. If the government of my country had evidence of UFOs, I'm sure they would tell us.

7. Aliens

Practice and Discussion

PERSONALIZATION

Complete these sentences with your own ideas.

It is arrogant to assume that …
I've been looking for … for years.
If there are intelligent aliens …
… should be able to … by now.
There's probably evidence that shows that …
Governments keep … secret.
I'm not ready to …
The government of my country wouldn't …

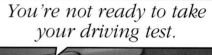

> You're not ready to take your driving test.

"Why did you come to Earth in a UFO?"
"It was too far to walk."

DISCUSSION

> That's what I was trying to say, but I couldn't express myself very well.

Try to include the discussion strategies and the patterns from the personalization section in the following discussions.

Do you think there is a lot of intelligent life in the universe? Why?
Do you know any stories of UFO sightings?
Do you think democratic governments keep secrets from us? For example?
What will be the next stages of humans' exploration of space?
When do you think humans will be able to travel around the universe? How?
How does the human race need to develop before doing this successfully?
Do you think humans might be descended from aliens? Why?

Activities

FOLLOW-UP QUESTIONS

List three things you think an alien might want to know about the Earth.

Example: What kind of food we eat.

Now talk to another student and ask at least two follow-up questions about each point.

Examples:

A: Why do you think an alien would want to know what food we eat?

B: She may be wondering if she can survive on Earth.

A: Don't you think she would bring her own food?

B: Yes, but she might want to live with us.

ROLE PLAY

Student A: *You are an interviewer. Interview an alien that has just landed on Earth.*

Student B: *You are the alien.*

Example questions:

Where are you from?

Why have you come here?

What kind of planet do you come from?

SITUATION - AN ALIEN WITH PROBLEMS

Brainstorming: *Think of problems an alien might have on Earth.*
Think of ways you could help an alien.
Think of what an alien could teach us.

Student A: *You are an alien who is having many problems on Earth.*
Student B: *Try to help A.*

Take turns to be A and B in the following situations.

1.   You broke your leg getting out of your UFO.
2.   You are at a gas station and want to buy gas for your UFO.
3.   You are homesick.
4.   You have met a cow who reminds you of an alien from back home. You wonder why the cow is not saying very much.
5.   You want to buy a new steering wheel for your UFO but are not sure where to buy one.
6.   You were expecting to be treated with great respect when you landed on Earth, but because of the size of your planet you are only the size of an ant on Earth.

"How did you break your leg?"
"You see those steps in front of my UFO?"
"Yes."
"Well, I didn't."

7. Aliens

Further Activities

COLLOCATION SETS

Put the following into sentences or dialogues.

Space
1. space exploration   *Example:*   The exploration of space must continue until we have found other intelligent life.

2. not enough space to
3. give ... space

Solar
1. solar energy   *Example:*   Eventually, solar energy will replace other forms of energy.
2. solar system
3. solar powered

Mystery
1. a complete mystery   *Example:*   Whether or not ghosts exist is a complete mystery.
2. an unsolved mystery
3. remain a mystery

SPEECHES

Prepare a short speech on one of these three topics.

We are descended from aliens.
There are aliens living on the Earth now, probably disguised as
   humans.
Aliens hide from humans because we are so aggressive and primitive.

EXTRA EXPRESSIONS

Put the following into short dialogues.

You're not serious!   Don't ask me!
make fun of   Your guess is as good as
               mine.

Example:
A: What do you think that bright light is?
B: Your guess is as good as mine.

*"What's yellow and white and travels through
the universe at 10,000 light years per second?"*
"Don't ask me!"
"An egg sandwich in a UFO."

Consolidation & Recycling

BUILDING VOCABULARY

Across

1   We could travel through space by shifting into another ___.
5   It'll keep me on my ___.
7   We should use less ___ fuels.
8   We need to stop using ___ chemicals.
11   Good teachers are ___ to all students.
13   We must act soon to ___ any chance of success.
14   Do you think aliens have visited the ___?
15   Your guess is as good as ___.
17   Let's save it for a ___ day.
18   Aliens don't visit us because humans are too ___.
20   The teachers must ___ through the syllabus.
24   I need to practice speaking English for my ___ exam.
25   We had a lot of ___ of choice.
26   I want to find things out for ___.
27   He had no ___ to commit the crime.

Down

1   Cutting down forests.
2   It will remain an unsolved ___.
3   ___-motivation.
4   Looking on the bright side.
6   It must ___ like I read too much fiction.
9   I don't know if I'm coming ___ going.
10   The world's climate is ___.
12   It sent a ___ down my spine.
13   Some governments keep their knowledge ___.
16   The Solar ___.
19   The aliens come from another ___.
21   You'd better ___ the police.
22   They are ___ outer space.
23   I'm in ___ and need to borrow money.

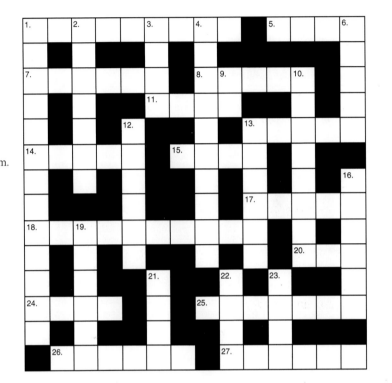

FOCUSING ON COLLOCATIONS

Write eight separate sentences, each of which includes both words in the pairs below.

solar / energy
human / race
price / range
guess / mine

space / exploration
mature / student
complete / mystery
breathtaking / view

WRITING OPINIONS

Write paragraphs about the following. Try to include words and patterns from this unit.

Is there intelligent life on other planets?
If I met an alien.
An SF movie I've seen/An SF novel I've read.

REFLECTION

Which section of the unit did you find most interesting?
In which section of the unit did you learn the most?
Make a list of any new words and patterns from this unit that you want to try and remember.
You may find it helpful to write each word or pattern on a card.

8. History

WARM-UP QUESTIONS

Name one event that happened in each of the following periods. List the things you know about that event.

2000 B.C. - 500 A.D.
500 A.D. - 1500 A.D.
1500 A.D. - 1800 A.D.
1800 A.D. - 1950 A.D.

VOCABULARY

Here are some words and expressions that will be useful in this unit.
How many do you know?

ancient	innovation	colonies
period	Renaissance	feudal system
civil war	aristocracy	reform
medieval	Industrial Revolution	civilization

Discuss which of the above words and expressions could fit in the following gaps.

Francesca: I wish I could have lived during the ____. It would have been wonderful to see the old ways of the ____ ____, such as the ____, being challenged and reformed. I might even have met a great artist like Michelangelo or Leonardo da Vinci!

Carlos: The reality was probably pretty horrible. There may have been a lot of ____ going on around you, but you probably would have been sick most of the time unless, perhaps, you were a member of the ____, and even then you would have been constantly caught up in wars with other countries or in some ____.

Francesca: I guess it wasn't until the ____ that modern society developed, and even that was paid for by suffering in factories in the industrializing countries, and by the exploitation of people in ____. So, despite the problems we have today, at least we live healthier and happier lives.

What words and expressions that are not in the list can you think of that might be useful when talking about history?

MIND MAP

Here is Francesca's mind map starting from 'life 500 years ago'.

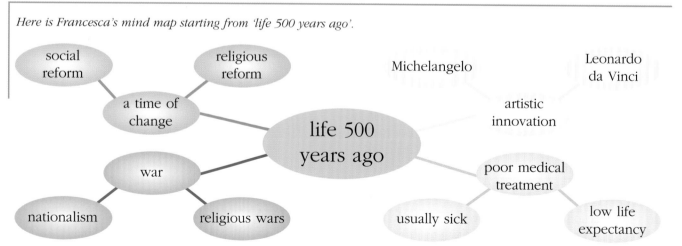

Now make your own mind map with 'life 500 years ago', 'life in ancient times', 'life in the nineteenth century', or 'famous historical figures' in the center. Talk about your mind map with another student or the rest of the class.

Waterloo - De Laurentiis/Mosfilm

POINTS OF VIEW - I ADMIRE NAPOLEON

The person in history I admire most is Napoleon. He wasn't just a great general. He also introduced a legal system that's still the basis of modern European law. He must have been a great leader of men, too. I've heard he could remember the names of ordinary soldiers even when he hadn't seen them for years.

Why do you men always respect generals or admirals or people who were responsible for so much killing and suffering? The person I respect most is Florence Nightingale. She started a great nursing tradition and did so much to take care of all the suffering caused by famous male generals and male politicians. If countries at that time had been run by women like her, there wouldn't have been any wars in the first place.

That's a very sweeping statement! Wars are not usually caused by individuals. And female leaders have often been just as aggressive as male leaders, if not more so. How about Catherine the Great of Russia or Margaret Thatcher?

That's because they were leaders in a society created by men. If more of our society was controlled by women, we would live in a much more humane and peaceful world. And it's not just me who says this. You talk to the wives and mothers of all the men who die in senseless wars started by male politicians.

8. History

Practice and Discussion

PERSONALIZATION

Complete these sentences with your own ideas.

... must have been a ...
I've heard ... even when ...
... did so much ...
If governments in the past had been run by women ...
If ... in the first place.
Wars are usually caused by ...
If ... we would live in a much more humane world.
If more of our society was controlled by women ...

I've heard he gets angry even when we make small mistakes.

"Where was the American Declaration of Independence signed?"
"At the bottom."

DISCUSSION

It may seem like he's the boss, but, in fact, it's the other way around.

DISCUSSION STRATEGIES

It's not only/just me who says this.
That's a very sweeping statement.
It's the other way around.

Try to include the discussion strategies and the patterns from the personalization section in the following discussions.

Which historical figure do you admire most? Why?

What lessons can we learn from history?

How do you think history would have been different if women had been more powerful in the past?

How might the world be different if there had been no Industrial Revolution, American War of Independence, Second World War, communist revolution in China, or British Empire?

How can we create a more humane and peaceful world?

Activities

FOLLOW-UP QUESTIONS

List three problems ordinary people had to face one thousand years ago.

Example: They would probably only live a short time.

Now talk to another student and ask at least two follow-up questions about each point.

Examples:

A: Why would they only live a short time?

B: Because they could easily become sick or be killed in a war.

A: Wouldn't a doctor help them if they became sick?

B: Maybe, but doctors didn't have enough medical knowledge in those days.

ROLE PLAY

Student A: *You are a famous person in history (choose which one).*

Student B: *You are a time traveler. Ask Student A questions.*

Example questions:
Which of your plays is your favorite?
How did you become the leader of the revolution?
Why did you decide to live in Tahiti?

SITUATION - TO FIGHT OR NOT TO FIGHT

Brainstorming: *Think of reasons why you might fight in a war.*
Think of reasons against fighting in a war.
Think of how ordinary people a hundred years ago could have avoided fighting when ordered to do so by their government.

Student A: *You are living a hundred years ago. The leaders of your country have decided to attack another country. You believe it is the duty of everybody to fight.*

Examples:
It is our patriotic duty to fight for our country.
We should fight for the sake of our families and friends.
If you don't fight, you may be shot or sent to prison.

Student B: *You are the brother/sister of Student A. You are against war, don't want to fight, and definitely believe it is wrong to attack another country.*

Examples:
We are being controlled by generals and politicians.
They don't care about people like us.
Maybe I could work in a hospital helping people wounded in the fighting.
War is always wrong. Patriotism just makes people blind.

"What did you say to the princess after you rescued her from the dragon?"
"May I put my armor round you?"

8. History

Further Activities

COLLOCATION SETS

Put the following into sentences or dialogues.

History

1. rewrite history

Example: In some countries, school textbook writers are trying to rewrite history.

2. change the course of history
3. history repeats itself

Period

1. honeymoon period

Example: At first there was a honeymoon period when everybody worked together, but it didn't last long.

2. Reformation period
3. a difficult period

War

1. threat of war

Example: Governments often believe that the threat of war is an effective deterrent.

2. war ... break out
3. a war memorial

SPEECHES

Prepare a short speech on one of these three topics.

We should look at the present and the future, not the past.
History is never fair. It's usually written by the victors or most powerful.
We are much wiser and live in a much better society than people in the past.

EXTRA EXPRESSIONS

Put the following into short dialogues.

once bitten twice shy   only/just a matter of time
there's no going back now   try, try, and try again

Example:

A: I can't understand why I ever agreed to write this book.

B: Well, there's no going back now. You signed the contract.

"What did the Greeks say when they were tired of attacking Troy?"
"Troy, Troy, and Troy again!"

Consolidation & Recycling

BUILDING VOCABULARY

Across

1   That's a very ___ statement!
6   The ___ penalty.
7   A ___ of the tongue.
8   A black ___.
9   You ___ your health by eating all that junk food.
11   There's no ___ difference in the murder rates.
13   Teachers should ___ students learn.
14   We were able to ___ out of court.
15   That should keep them on ___ toes.
17   He was ___ to prison.
18   There's a large building that ___ the view.
21   We need to ___ things for ourselves.
22   They keep their ___ secret.
23   I hope the UN ___ up a new organization.

Down

1   There have been many ___ of UFOs.
2   The ___ of poorer countries by richer ones.
3   There was a lot ___ on around me.
4   We need ___ to start a new business.
5   I can't change my ___! I know I'm negative and pessimistic!
7   So many people die in ___ wars.
10   Name one ___ that happened in the 15th century.
12   Arresting me meant ___ me as a criminal.
16   I'd like to ___ some money in a profitable company.
18   There's no going ___ now.
19   Murderers shouldn't be set free to ___ more innocent people.
20   Business is bad so we may make a ___.

FOCUSING ON COLLOCATIONS

Write eight separate sentences, each of which includes both words in the pairs below.

life / expectancy

speed / light

war / break

education / system

rewrite / history

adapt / environment

lateral / thinking

matter / time

WRITING OPINIONS

Write paragraphs about the following. Try to include words and patterns from this unit.

People in history who have impressed me most.

Is war ever necessary?

Lessons to be learned from history.

REFLECTION

Which section of the unit did you find most interesting?

In which section of the unit did you learn the most?

Make a list of any new words and patterns from this unit that you want to try and remember.

You may find it helpful to write each word or pattern on a card.

9. Women in Society

WARM-UP QUESTIONS

Think of five non-physical ways you think men and women may be different.
Do you think they are born with these differences? If not, what causes them?
Do you think men and women should be treated equally? Why?
In which jobs do you think men and women are treated most equally?

VOCABULARY

Here are some words and expressions that will be useful in this unit.
How many do you know?

discrimination	appropriate	genetically
careers	sexual harassment	sexist
quota	equal opportunities	social customs
affirmative action	male-dominated	conditioned

Discuss which of the above words and expressions could fit in the following gaps.

Tomoko: Our society is so ____. People talk about ____, but, in fact, men have all the power. In many jobs, they can even get away with ____ of female employees and all kinds of ____ comments.

Chen: I think that's partly because some women want to have ____ in occupations more suited to men. We should accept that we are ____ different. There is very little ____ in jobs that are more ____ for women.

Tomoko: How can you say that! Even in most of those jobs, a higher percentage of managers are men. And the jobs you imagine are more ____ for men only appear so because of ____ created by men. We need ____ to ensure there's a ____ of female managers in all major companies.

What words and expressions that are not in the list can you think of that might be useful when talking about men and women?

MIND MAP

Here is Tomoko's mind map starting from 'discrimination against women'.

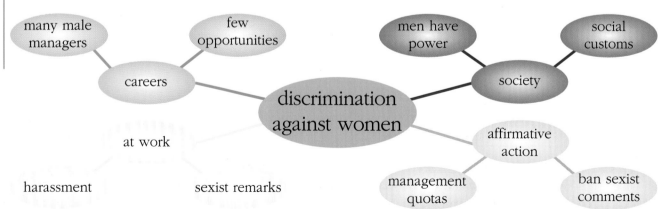

Now make your own mind map with 'discrimination against women', 'the changing role of men', 'affirmative action', or 'sexual harassment'. Talk about your mind map with another student or the rest of the class.

Erin Brockovich - Universal, ph: Bob Marshak

POINTS OF VIEW - WOMEN DON'T HAVE THE SAME OPPORTUNITIES AS MEN

It's very hard being a woman sometimes! We're supposed to be equal to men, but we just don't have the same opportunities. And most men still expect us to do the housework and take care of the children even when we have full-time jobs. When I was married, I went out once a month at most.

I don't agree. There are a lot of women in top management positions, and there are plenty of opportunities for women who are interested in having a career. Many of the women who don't have responsible jobs are often happy to support their male bosses or pay more attention to their families.

At first I thought the same way, but after working in an office for a while, I realized that way of thinking is just an illusion that's convenient for men. The reason why many women don't want responsibility is simply that they are conditioned to think that way from the moment they are born. It's such a waste! And it's not true that there are plenty of opportunities for women. It's very hard for us to get to the top, and there's a lot of discrimination and sexual harassment along the way.

Well, at least things are better than they used to be.

9. Women in Society

Practice and Discussion

PERSONALIZATION

Complete these sentences with your own ideas.

It's very hard …
I'm supposed to be …
Most women expect men to …
I should pay more attention to …
… is just an illusion.
I've been conditioned to think that …
… such a waste!
There's a lot of discrimination …

It's very hard to work out every day.

"Where have you been all my life?"
"For most of it I wasn't even born."

DISCUSSION

If I ask him out, the worst that can happen is that he'll say 'no'.

DISCUSSION STRATEGIES

at least/at most
at first/at last
the best/worst that can happen is

Try to include the discussion strategies and the patterns from the personalization section in the following discussions.

How do you feel about husbands who expect working wives to do most of the housework?
How can more opportunities be created for women who want to have a career?
Are many women happy supporting men? If so, why?
Are the roles of men and women conditioned by society?
What do you think it means to be 'feminine' and 'masculine'?
How much sexual harassment is there at work? For example?
If you could choose, would you prefer to be a man or a woman? Why?

Activities

FOLLOW-UP QUESTIONS

List three things you think it is more socially acceptable for either a man to do than a woman or a woman to do than a man.

Example: It's more acceptable for a woman to cry.

Now talk to another student and ask at least two follow-up questions about each point.

Examples:

A: Do you think it's still true?

B: Yes, especially at work or with strangers.

A: Don't you think others will care or try to help if a man cries?

B: I think most other people will see him as strange or weak.

ROLE PLAY

Student A: *You are applying for a job that is normally done by a member of the opposite sex. Persuade Student A that you can do the job well.*

Student B: *You are interviewing Student A.*

Example questions:

Are you sure you could handle it? You'd have to ...

How would you feel if your boss and co-workers were all female?

Why do you think you can do this job as well as a man/woman?

SITUATION - BOASTING

Brainstorming: *Think of personal or physical qualities you'd like a boyfriend or girlfriend to have.*
Think of things you'd like a boyfriend or girlfriend to be able to do.

Students A and B:
Boast about your girlfriend/boyfriend (real or imaginary). Try to outdo each other.

After doing this, look at some of the things you said and see if there are things you would say about girlfriends and not boyfriends, or vice versa.

Examples:

Whenever I'm depressed, he always tries to cheer me up.

She has a great sense of humor.

He's one of the best tennis players in ...

I bet my girlfriend can ... better than your girlfriend.

"So, what did you think of humans?"
"Well, I liked the intelligent ones, but I didn't think much of the ones that had most of the top jobs."

9. Women in Society

Further Activities

COLLOCATION SETS

Put the following into sentences or dialogues.

Opportunity
1. every opportunity   *Example:*   He takes every opportunity to boast about his new job.
2. waste an opportunity
3. a window of opportunity

Sexual
1. sexual harassment   *Example:*   Almost all female office workers suffer sexual harassment from time to time.

2. sexual discrimination
3. sexual innuendo

Man
1. right-hand man   *Example:*   If I play my cards right, I'll become the President's right-hand man.
2. middle-aged man
3. self-made man

SPEECHES

Prepare a short speech on one of these three topics.

Women should stay home and look after the children.
Men are naturally more aggressive than women.
Women are too vain.

EXTRA EXPRESSIONS

Put the following into short dialogues.

a woman's place is in the   diamonds are a girl's best
   home   friend
take for granted   male chauvinist

Example:
A: So many men take women for granted and don't realize it until they're not there.
B: I think women sometimes take men for granted, too.

"Diamonds are a girl's best friend."
"Dogs are a man's best friend."
"So who's the smartest?"

Consolidation & Recycling

BUILDING VOCABULARY

Across
1   We have to ___ that we are different.
7   We should study at home by ___.
8   The ___ system existed in the Middle Ages.
9   New technology may ___ us to travel through space.
11   You run the ___ of losing a lot of money.
12   I wish all countries were ___ by women like her.
13   I want to find ___ out for myself.
16   It was a slip of the ___.
18   Things are better than they ___ to be.
19   Liked by many people.
20   There should be ___ opportunities for women.
21   Could aliens be living ___ us?
22   I find it tough to ___ a living.
24   I often sneeze when there's ___ in the air.
25   ___ space.

Down
1   ___ action.
2   It could change the ___ of history.
3   I can't ___ any of my boyfriend's flirting.
4   Teachers should ___ students equally.
5   I wish she would stop ___ me what to do.
6   I couldn't ___ away with it.
10   This food only has natural ___.
14   Their conversations are full of sexual ___.
15   I wonder what the main ___ of pollution is.
17   ___ habitat.
19   There wouldn't have been any wars in the first ___.
23   We have to stop polluting the ___.

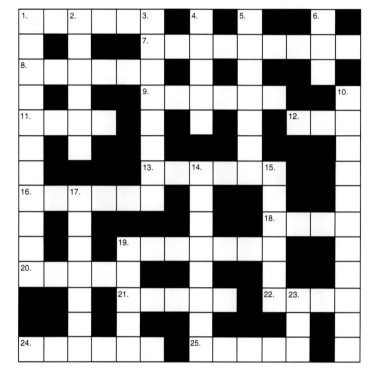

FOCUSING ON COLLOCATIONS

Write eight separate sentences, each of which includes both words in the pairs below.

equal / opportunities	middle-aged / man
patriotic / duty	higher / percentage
solar / system	crime / rate
waste / opportunity	natural / habitat

WRITING OPINIONS

Write paragraphs about the following. Try to include words and patterns from this unit.

The position of women in society.
The advantages and disadvantages of being female.
The similarities and differences between men and women.

REFLECTION

Which section of the unit did you find most interesting?
In which section of the unit did you learn the most?
Make a list of any new words and patterns from this unit that you want to try and remember.
You may find it helpful to write each word or pattern on a card.

10. The Developing W

WARM-UP QUESTIONS

Do you think most people in your country are rich or poor?
Is it fair that people in some countries are much richer than people in others?
What do you think the causes of this are?
Do you think anything can be done to improve the situation? If so, what?

VOCABULARY

Here are some words and expressions that will be useful in this unit.
How many do you know?

aid	birth control	corruption
charity	poverty	refugee
debts	United Nations	armed forces
hunger	donating	free trade

Discuss which of the above words and expressions could fit in the following gaps.

Francesca: What's the point of ____ ____ to developing countries? The governments spend
so much of it on their ____ and do very little to reduce ____ and ____. And
the government bureaucracies that administer the ____ are riddled with ____.

Christina: There are many people in developing countries and at the ____ who are trying to fight these problems.
The worst thing we can do is sit back and say problems like ____ and ____ cannot be solved, or ignore
all the people in ____ camps who need our help.

Francesca: I think developing countries should first focus on ____ programs, reducing government ____, and
revitalizing their economies. Then we can consider ____ and ____.

*What words and expressions that are not in the list can you think of that might be useful when talking about the
developing world?*

MIND MAP

Here is Francesca's mind map starting from 'developing countries'.

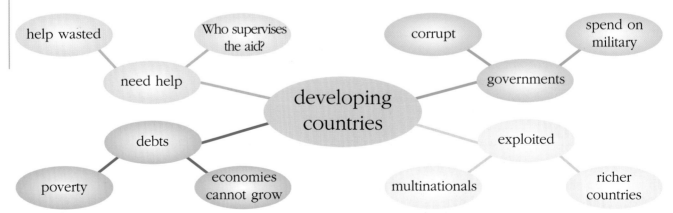

Now make your own mind map with 'developing countries', 'what our countries can do', 'what we can do', or 'free trade'.
Talk about your mind map with another student or the rest of the class.

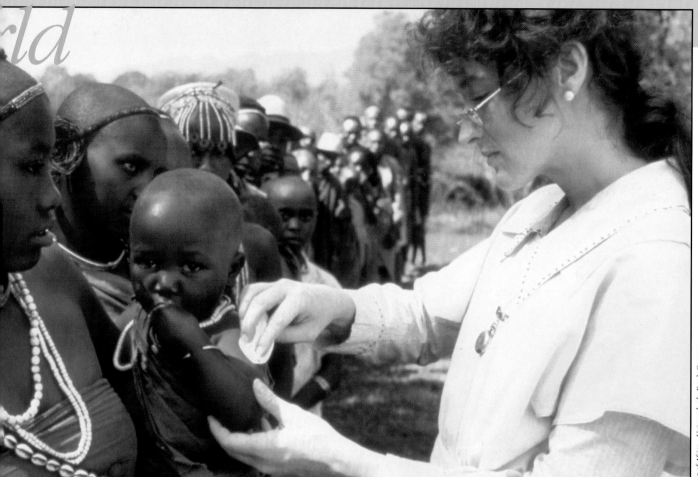

Out of Africa – Universal, ph: Frank Connor

POINTS OF VIEW - FREE TRADE MAKES EVERYBODY RICHER

I believe in free trade. If every country in the world reduced import barriers, the world economy would grow and we'd all be richer.

Only the rich countries and the multinationals would be better off. Free trade makes the rich richer and the poor poorer. It prevents developing countries from being able to protect their industries until they are strong enough to compete globally. What you're really saying is that you want the western economies and Japan to continue controlling the world.

Of course I'm not saying that. What I'm saying is that a strong world economy benefits everybody. For example, it makes it easier for the wealthier countries to provide aid to developing countries. The multinationals will also have more capital to invest in building factories in poorer countries, and this will provide well-paid jobs.

Countries that give aid usually insist that most of it is spent on goods that they export. This means the aid often does more harm than good. It stops local industries from developing. And the multinationals only want to have factories in developing countries because they don't have to pay high salaries. As soon as local salaries increase too much, they move their factories to other countries.

Unit 10: The Developing World • 63

Practice and Discussion

PERSONALIZATION

Complete these sentences with your own ideas.

If every country in the world …
I could become better off by …
… make(s) …
… stop(s) …
If … it will provide well-paid jobs.
My teacher/boss insists …
… do(es) more harm than good.
The multinationals only want …

> *My boss insists that I do overtime every day.*

"What's this?"
"It's bean soup."
"Yes, but what is it now?"

DISCUSSION

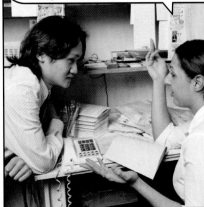

> *So, I should just quit! That's easy to say! I have a son to support!*

DISCUSSION STRATEGIES

What … saying is …
… not saying …
That's easy to say.

Try to include the discussion strategies and the patterns from the controlled practice section in the following discussions.

What would be the effect if all countries reduced import barriers?
If the world economy gets stronger, to what extent do you think people in developing countries will benefit?
How can aid to developing countries be made more effective?
To what extent do you think multinationals exploit developing countries?
How do you think local industries in developing countries can be built up?
Does there have to be a big change in the attitudes of people in richer countries?
What can each of us do to help more?

Activities

FOLLOW-UP QUESTIONS

List three ways that individuals in richer countries can help people in developing countries.

Example: We can give part of our income to charity.

Now talk to another student and ask at least two follow-up questions about each point.

Examples:

A: Would you really be prepared to give some of your income to charity?

B: Yes, I already do, though only 10% .

A: Do you think it gets through to people who need it?

B: Yes, I'm careful about which charities I donate money to.

ROLE PLAY

Student A: You are the leader of a developing country asking Student A for help.

Student B: You are the leader of a wealthy country. You want to help, but Student A's country has a bad human rights record, and there is a lot of government corruption.

Example questions:

How do we know the money will get through to the people who need it?

If we build hospitals, could they be run by the Red Cross?

SITUATION - PLANNING A FACTORY

Brainstorming: Think of the risks a company may take when building a factory in a developing country.
Think of the advantages the company may look for.
Think of how the government of the country may try to ensure that the factory benefits local people and the local economy.

Student A: You are the president of a company that is thinking of building a factory in a developing country.

Examples:

Will we get a government subsidy or tax exemptions?

You'd have to guarantee that we could keep salaries and hourly pay rates low.

Would we be able to get loans easily?

Student B: You are a leader of that country. You badly need the factory, but you also want to protect local people.

Examples:

No children would be allowed to work in the factory.

You would only need to pay taxes on exports.

50% of the managers would have to be local.

"Can't you see the sign! It says 'NO SWIMMING!'"
"I'm not swimming. I'm drowning!"
"Oh. Well, that's all right then."

Further Activities

COLLOCATION SETS

Put the following into sentences or dialogues.

Aid
1. emergency aid   *Example:*   Last week many countries rushed emergency aid to the survivors of the earthquake.

2. in need of aid
3. appeal for aid

Poverty
1. reduce poverty   *Example:*   The government has been trying to reduce poverty, but with little success.
2. widespread poverty
3. poverty line

Charity
1. go to charity   *Example:*   All the proceeds from her next album will go to charity.
2. a registered charity
3. charity begins at home

SPEECHES

Prepare a short speech on one of these three topics.

Developing countries are poor because of colonial exploitation.
People in developing countries should work harder and have fewer children.
Developing countries should cut military spending and reduce corruption before expecting help from rich countries.

EXTRA EXPRESSIONS

Put the following into short dialogues.

go through a hard time   every little bit helps
could be worse   something's better than nothing

Example:
A: Things could be worse. We might have no place to sleep.
B: They couldn't get much worse. I'm hungry!

"You look as though you've been through a famine."
"You look as though you caused it!"

Consolidation & Recycling

BUILDING VOCABULARY

Across

1. It blocks imports.
6. There's widespread ___ in developing countries.
8. Men and women should be treated ___.
9. ___ rain.
10. Very old.
11. I wish women would ___ a new society.
13. It's not a ___ injury.
17. Many doctors are ___ servants.
18. I wonder if UFOs ___.
20. I wish that were ___.
21. The earthquake caused a big ___.
22. There's usually a ___ period at the beginning.

Down

1. The government ___ makes aid less effective.
2. A person who escapes from their country.
3. We need to ___ more money to charity.
4. Free ___ hurts developing countries.
5. Increasing tax would make the economy less ___.
7. We have to find a ___ that can support human life.
10. There were no girls ___ all.
12. She has a very responsible ___.
14. There's no ___ ___ just leaving it in the bank.
15. You're not ___!
16. We are in ___ and need to borrow more money.
19. They can't see the forest for the ___.
20. Some doctors prescribe ___ much medicine.

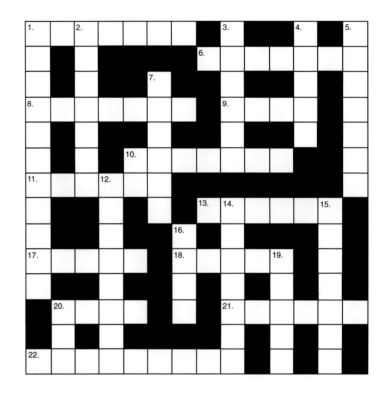

FOCUSING ON COLLOCATIONS

Write eight separate sentences, each of which includes both words in the pairs below.

need / aid
poverty / line
free / trade
sexual / discrimination

take / granted
male / dominated
difficult / period
something / nothing

WRITING OPINIONS

Write paragraphs about the following. Try to include words and patterns from this unit.

A country in need.
What individuals in richer countries can do to help developing countries.
What the governments of richer countries can do.

REFLECTION

Which section of the unit did you find most interesting?
In which section of the unit did you learn the most?
Make a list of any new words and patterns from this unit that you want to try and remember.
You may find it helpful to write each word or pattern on a card.

11. Violence

WARM-UP QUESTIONS

Do you think the amount of violence in society is increasing or decreasing? Why?
Do you ever feel afraid when you walk around the streets near where you live? Why?
Where do you think you might feel more afraid? Why?
Why do you think some people are more violent than others?

VOCABULARY

*Here are some words and expressions that will be useful in this unit.
How many do you know?*

hostages	aggressive	vandalism
serial killer	sensationalize	victims
shocking	role models	outlet
threaten	revenge	terrorism

Discuss which of the above words and expressions could fit in the following gaps.

Annan: Violence has become a normal part of modern society. Every day we hear news of murders, ____, ____ being taken ... Sometimes criminals single out innocent ____ and shoot them in cold blood. Even children commit these kinds of horrible crimes.

Nazim: It's certainly true that we live in a very ____ world, but don't you think we find it so ____ because most of us live peaceful, law-abiding lives? In the past, people were surrounded by aggression and war, but, these days, most of us just watch it on TV.

Annan: The situation may have got better before it got worse. When I was a child, I could walk the streets around my house at night, and the TV and movie stars who were ____ for young people were not so outwardly ____, and there was less ____ of public property.

What words and expressions that are not in the list can you think of that might be useful when talking about violence?

MIND MAP

Here is Annan's mind map starting from 'increasing violence'.

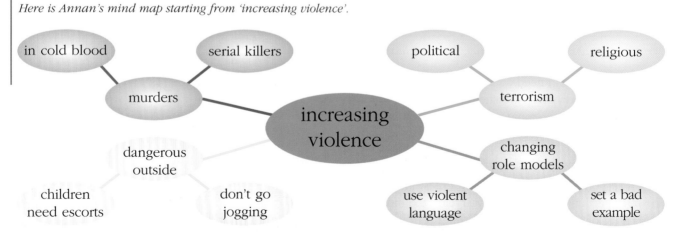

*Now make your own mind map with 'increasing violence', 'terrorism', 'outlets for violence', or 'role models' in the center.
Talk about your mind map with another student or the rest of the class.*

Ali - Columbia, ph: Frank Connor

POINTS OF VIEW - VIOLENT SPORTS SHOULD BE BANNED

Violent sports like boxing and wrestling should be banned. They set a bad example, especially to children. They send out a message that it's all right to fight and hit people. If we banned these kinds of sports, I'm sure there'd be fewer wars, less violent crime, and less school bullying.

That's a nice argument, but I think you'd find it hard to prove, and not many people would support you. Boxing and wrestling are traditional sports which a lot of people enjoy. I think we should also accept that there's going to be a certain amount of violence in society whatever we do, and it's better if a sport provides an outlet for this violence. Sports can act as a substitute for more direct aggression and even war.

There's a lot of evidence to suggest that violent crime increases immediately after a televised heavyweight boxing match.

That says more about the media than it does about boxing or wrestling. Violence increases after violent movies are shown on TV, and the number of suicides increases after the media gives heavy publicity to a suicide story. It's unfair to ban physical sports just because the media is irresponsible. If the media didn't sensationalize the violence in these sports, there wouldn't be any problem.

11. Violence

Practice and Discussion

PERSONALIZATION

Complete these sentences with your own ideas.

> ... set(s) a bad example.
> ... send(s) out a message that ...
> It's hard to prove ...
> There's going to be ... whatever we do.
> ... provide(s) an outlet for ...
> ... can act as a substitute for ...
> The media gives heavy publicity to ...
> ... sensationalize(s) ...

If people smoke on TV, it sends out a message that it's cool to smoke.

"Yesterday afternoon a prison bus rammed a cement mixer. The police are looking for sixteen hardened criminals."

DISCUSSION

When you warn me not to ask her out, it just tells me a lot about how jealous you are.

DISCUSSION STRATEGIES

... a nice argument, but ...
... tells me a lot about ...
... says more about ...

Try to include the discussion strategies and the patterns from the personalization section in the following discussions.

Do you think violent sports should be banned? Why?

Do people need outlets for violent instincts? If so, what can provide these outlets?

Do you think sport is often a modern substitute for war? Why?

Is the media responsible for a lot of the increase in violence in society? Why?

How can we prevent children from regarding violence as normal?

How do you think the amount of violence in our society can be reduced?

How do you think war and terrorism can be reduced?

Activities

FOLLOW-UP QUESTIONS

List three ways in which the media can influence our behavior and opinions.

Example: The media selects the news we hear about.

Now talk to another student and ask at least two follow-up questions about each point.

Examples:

A: Don't you think it's natural that they select the news?
B: Yes, but they tend to select the most sensational and entertaining news.
A: What's wrong with that?
B: It makes us think it's normal for life to be more sensational than it needs to be.

ROLE PLAY

Student A: *You are Martin Luther King. You have just said 'You try to provoke me to threaten violence, and, if I don't, then you will put on television those who do. And by putting them on television, you will elect them our leaders.'*

Student B: *Interview Martin Luther King just after he made the above statement.*

Example questions:

Why do you think the media tries to provoke you to threaten violence?
Why will those who threaten violence become our leaders?

SITUATION - MAKING EXCUSES

Brainstorming: *Think of questions a police officer might ask somebody who is carrying a hand grenade.*
Think of innocent reasons for having a hand grenade.
Think of follow-up questions for each of these reasons.

Student A: *You are a kidnapper who has been stopped by the police. You have to think of reasons for having the following things with you: a suitcase full of money, a photograph of the person who has just been kidnapped, a large bag of food, a pile of newspapers with words cut out, a knife, a gun, and a hand grenade.*

Examples:

Isn't it a nice picture? I just found it.
I can't write very well, so I cut out words from the newspaper.
I have to defend myself. The city's very dangerous these days.

Student B: *You are the police office who has just stopped Student A.*

Examples:

Haven't I seen that photograph somewhere before?
Where did you get $1,000,000?
Are you planning to start a war?

"Why are you pointing that gun at your corn flakes?"
"I'm a cereal killer."

11. Violence

Further Activities

COLLOCATION SETS

Put the following into sentences or dialogues.

Violence
1. resort to violence
2. violence … escalating
3. outburst of violence

Example: I only resort to violence as a last resort.

Hit
1. hit it off
2. hit the nail on the head
3. hit on a good idea

Example: As soon as I set eyes on him, I knew we were going to hit it off.

Fight
1. fight for
2. prepared to fight
3. have a fight on … hands

Example: We are fighting for our freedom.

SPEECHES

Prepare a short speech on one of these three topics.

It is never right to fight, even to defend one's country.
One man's terrorists are another man's freedom fighters.
Sex and violence in advertising and the media should be strictly
   controlled.

EXTRA EXPRESSIONS

Put the following into short dialogues.

Calm down!   Stay out of it!
Keep quiet!   Mind your own business!

Example:
A: Who was that girl I saw you with yesterday?
B: Mind your own business!

"Keep quiet! Order in court!"
"I'll have an egg sandwich, please."

Consolidation & Recycling

BUILDING VOCABULARY

Across

1   ___ aid had to be rushed to the disaster area.
4   Is it ___ that some people have much more than others?
6   Potential criminals should spend time ___ the consequences of their actions.
8   Teachers should let students ___.
9   Most of us live peaceful ___.
10 It's hard to get to the ___.
12 All countries need to ___ on international policies.
13 The ___ Revolution.
15 An ___ mystery.
18 It's just a ___ of time.
20 He was shot in ___ blood.
22 ___ bitten twice shy.
23 Every day we hear ___ of murders.
24 People at that time had a ___ life expectancy.

Down

1   Becoming more and more.
2   I only ___ to violence when there's no other way.
3   The government is riddled with ___.
5   I only trust ___ charities.
7   ___ little bit helps.
11 It's arrogant to ___ we are the only intelligent beings.
12 As well.
14 We need to take ___ action.
16 It ___ out a message that it's all right to fight.
17 In that area or region.
19 We ___ the risk of losing our money.
21 It's against the ___.

FOCUSING ON COLLOCATIONS

Write eight separate sentences, each of which includes both words in the pairs below.

hit / idea
self / man
unsolved / mystery
violence / escalating

fight / for
honeymoon / period
court / case
mind / business

WRITING OPINIONS

Write paragraphs about the following. Try to include words and patterns from this unit.

Violent sports.
Violence on TV.
Is man an aggressive animal?

REFLECTION

Which section of the unit did you find most interesting?
In which section of the unit did you learn the most?
Make a list of any new words and patterns from this unit that you want to try and remember.
You may find it helpful to write each word or pattern on a card.

12. Politics

WARM-UP QUESTIONS

Would you like to be a politician? Why?
Which politicians do you like and dislike? Why?
What are the names of the main political parties in your country?
Say a little about each of them.

VOCABULARY

Here are some words and expressions that will be useful in this unit.
How many do you know?

moderate	interest groups	majority
socialist	election	represent
campaign	communism	idealists
left/right wing	Prime Minister	extremist

Discuss which of the above words and expressions could fit in the following gaps.

Manosh: I can't understand what politicians really want in life. Both conservative and ____ politicians seem so different from ordinary people, even though they claim to ____ us. Are they genuine ____, or do they just want power for its own sake and dream of becoming ____ or President some day?

Nazim: It must depend on the person. I generally trust ____ politicians more than ____ ones, but even many socialists or communists come across as insincere and consumed by ambition.

Manosh: I guess that's why ____ have so much influence. We're supposed to live in a democracy, but, in fact, for a political candidate to win a ____ in an ____, he or she has to manipulate people's opinions through a ____ that requires large sums of money supplied by ____. That's hardly democratic!

What words and expressions that are not in the list can you think of that might be useful when talking about politics?

MIND MAP

Here is Manosh's mind map starting from 'politicians'.

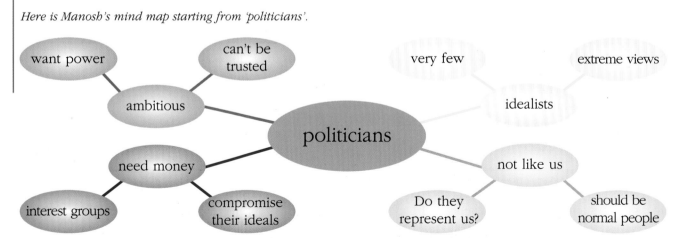

Now make your own mind map with 'politicians', 'a politician I respect', 'if I was a politician', or 'extremists'. Talk about your mind map with another student or the rest of the class.

The American President – Castle Rock/Universal/Wildwood, ph: Francois Duhamel

POINTS OF VIEW - THERE SHOULD BE NO EXTREMISTS

In my ideal country, there would be two main political parties. One would be moderately left-wing and the other moderately right-wing. There would be no extremists. There would be an election every four or five years, and the people would sometimes elect one of the parties and sometimes the other.

It doesn't sound very dynamic. What would happen if radical change was necessary? Don't you think it's a good idea to have extremists to keep the moderates on their toes? When political parties become too comfortable, they often become complacent and corrupt.

I don't think that's true. It's communist or military governments that tend to be the most corrupt. The system I'm suggesting would lead to sensible compromises on most contentious issues, and would work well as long as there was freedom of speech and freedom of the press to ensure that alternative points of view were fairly represented.

What if there was a major world crisis? I doubt if the politicians in your ideal country would be able to anticipate and deal with it. Everything would be controlled by career politicians and bureaucrats. And we need ideology and dynamic leadership in politics to give us all a sense of purpose. Your idea is very rational, but it's not inspiring enough.

12. Politics

Practice and Discussion

PERSONALIZATION

Complete these sentences with your own ideas.

In my country, there's an election …
… isn't/aren't very dynamic.
When radical change is necessary …
Many … are complacent.
… tend(s) to be corrupt.
… work(s) well.
… give(s) me a sense of purpose.
… isn't/aren't very inspiring.

"Nobody trusts me! They all think I'm lying."
"That's hard to believe."

DISCUSSION

DISCUSSION STRATEGIES

What would happen if … ?
What if … ?
How about if … ?

Try to include the discussion strategies and the patterns from the personalization section in the following discussions.

Describe and discuss your ideal political system.
How free and democratic is your country?
Can women, people without much money, and people from minority racial backgrounds easily become political leaders in your country? Why?
Which politicians in your country can anticipate and deal with crises?
How much power do bureaucrats have in your country?
What aspects of your society need radical change?

Activities

FOLLOW-UP QUESTIONS

List three qualities you think a good politician should have.

Example: A good politician should be compassionate.

Now talk to another student and ask at least two follow-up questions about each point.

Examples:

A: Why do you think a politician should be compassionate?

B: He or she should genuinely care about ordinary people.

A: Don't you think most politicians care?

B   Deep down they may care, but they get so involved in politics and their own careers that they forget to be compassionate.

ROLE PLAY

Student A: *You want to be Prime Minister or President of your country.*

Student B: *You are a newspaper interviewer trying to find out if Student A would be a good leader of your country.*

Example questions:

If you are elected, what would be the first thing you would do?

How would you improve the country's economy?

SITUATION - POLITICAL MANIFESTOS

If the class is big enough, get into pairs or groups, each of which is a different political party.

(1)   *There's going to be an election in Atlantis, an imaginary country in the middle of the Atlantic Ocean. Make a political manifesto for your party.*

Name your political party, and then make a list of your policies on: taxation, defence spending, health care, education, crime, and any other special issues you want to mention.

Examples:

People with an income below … will be exempt from paying income tax.

We will cut defence spending by 50%. We will achieve this mainly by getting rid of nuclear weapons.

We will double the size of the police force.

We will build more retirement homes for old people.

(2)   *Each pair/group should read out your manifesto. Then hold an election. The election could be preceded by a discussion or formal TV debate.*

Examples:

Where are you going to get the money to do that?

How can you reduce taxes and improve health care at the same time?

It sounds like we'll become a police state.

If we reduce defence spending so much, we'll probably be attacked by …

"If I become President, I'll stop bailing out the airlines."
"Why the airlines?"
"I've always disliked receding airlines."

12. Politics

Further Activities

COLLOCATION SETS

Put the following into sentences or dialogues.

Election
1. an election campaign

2. a fair election
3. a rigged election

Example: The recent election campaign was touch and go until the very end. We didn't know who would win until the last minute.

Vote
1. entitled to vote
2. unanimous vote
3. vote of no confidence

Example: Everybody over eighteen is entitled to vote.

Policy
1. foreign policy
2. government policy
3. economic policy

Example: The government needs to have clearer foreign policy objectives.

SPEECHES

Prepare a short speech on one of these three topics.

Business and powerful interest groups have the most political power.
There should be no countries. We should all have the same government, the same language, and the same currency.
There are no free countries in the world. We are all controlled by small elites of self-centered, ambitious politicians.

EXTRA EXPRESSIONS

Put the following into short dialogues.

behind ... back   pass the buck
delegate responsibility   take the credit

Example:
A: Somebody told me our teacher is going out with one of the school secretaries.
B: You shouldn't talk about people behind their backs! ... Which secretary?

"Now remember! A good politician is a team leader. You must learn to delegate as much work as possible. And then take the credit when things go well, and pass the buck when things go badly."

Consolidation & Recycling

BUILDING VOCABULARY

Across

1 A middle way.
8 People don't wear clothes in a ___ camp.
9 The ___ of the iceberg.
10 Be careful not to ___ your ankle!
11 There should be less vandalism of public ___.
13 Many people live below the poverty ___.
15 I ___ you would easily trust your partner.
16 Many people ___ of cancer.
17 We won with a unanimous ___.
19 In a democracy, we ___ our leaders.
22 How do you take care of ___ health?
24 Sports are an ___ for violence.
26 That's getting ___ from the point.
27 I sometimes ___ people in the heat of the moment.
28 It's a ___ of money.

Down

1 We need to find solutions to ___ issues.
2 Politicians ___ people's opinions.
3 It's hard to pay the ___ on this apartment.
4 Not extreme.
5 Very left wing or right wing.
6 Everbody over 18 is ___ to vote.
7 I ___ you aren't right!
12 My ambition is to become ___ Minister.
14 School textbooks sometimes ___ history.
18 There's more to it than meets the ___.
20 At ___ things are better than before.
21 Hard/difficult.
23 We have no right to take ___ human beings' lives.
25 I hope everything will ___ out OK.

FOCUSING ON COLLOCATIONS

Write eight separate sentences, each of which includes both words in the pairs below.

entitled / vote
prepared / fight
male / chauvinist
delegate / responsibility

pass / buck
appeal / aid
forest / trees
election / campaign

WRITING OPINIONS

Write paragraphs about the following. Try to include words and patterns from this unit.

A politician I respect.
My ideal political system.
The meaning of freedom.

REFLECTION

Which section of the unit did you find most interesting?
In which section of the unit did you learn the most?
Make a list of any new words and patterns from this unit that you want to try and remember.
You may find it helpful to write each word or pattern on a card.

13. Economics

WARM-UP QUESTIONS

Do you feel financially better off or worse off than two years ago? Why?
What are the current economic trends in your country?
Do you think your government is taking care of the economy well? Why?
What do you think are the biggest economic problems the world is facing?

VOCABULARY

Here are some words and expressions that will be useful in this unit.
How many do you know?

inflation	imports	Gross National Product
recession	market research	economic growth
indirect tax	productivity	consumption
exports	trade deficit	supply and demand

Discuss which of the above words and expressions could fit in the following gaps.

Carlos: The economy's in a mess. The ____ is getting larger, ____ is declining, and ____ is stagnating. If things get any worse, we'll be in ____.

Manosh: The government should do something. They always talk about the need for new, progressive ideas, and radical action, but it's just talk. They should encourage ____ so as to reduce the ____, and boost ____ so as to stimulate ____.

Carlos: They are always too cautious, and so afraid of ____. All the ____ that I've ever seen indicates that there's no serious danger of prices increasing too fast. We have to focus on avoiding ____.

What words and expressions that are not in the list can you think of that might be useful when talking about economics?

MIND MAP

Here is Carlos' mind map starting from 'the economy'.

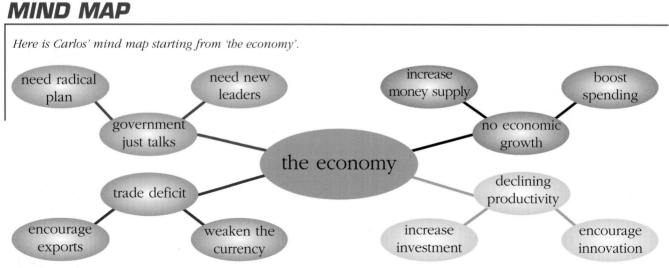

Now make your own mind map with 'the economy', 'taxes', 'the global economic situation', or 'the trade deficit' in the center. Talk about your mind map with another student or the rest of the class.

Rogue Trader - Capitol, ph: Paul Chedlow

POINTS OF VIEW - INCOME TAXES SHOULD BE REDUCED

If income taxes are reduced, everybody will have more money, and consumption will increase. If consumption increases, production will increase, too, so unemployment will fall.

When consumption increases, demand for goods increases, so companies put up prices. And when unemployment falls, there's pressure to increase pay. Both these factors lead to an increase in inflation.

But more people will be working, and it will give the economy a boost. GNP will be higher, so the government will get more income from indirect taxes. Everybody will be better off. The immediate effect of a reduction in income tax might be to cause inflation to rise slightly, but the long-term effects would benefit the economy.

Inflation hurts the poor more than the rich and leads to more unemployment in the long run. Personally, I think we should increase income taxes and reduce indirect taxes, such as taxes on consumption. Income tax can be progressive, so it affects the rich more than the poor and profitable companies more than the unprofitable ones, but indirect taxes affect everybody.

13. Economics

Practice and Discussion

PERSONALIZATION

Complete these sentences with your own ideas.

> If income taxes are increased …
> If consumption decreases …
> Unemployment will rise if …
> If GNP falls …
> High unemployment leads to …
> The government will get less income if …
> Higher income taxes would hurt …
> … affect(s) everybody.

If income taxes are increased, I may have to sell my bicycle.

"My new business is now secure. It has a very firm foundation."
"I see. You mean it's on the rocks."

DISCUSSION

If I eat less ice cream, I should lose weight in the long run.

DISCUSSION STRATEGIES

… in the long run …
… the long-term effect(s) …
… the immediate effect(s) …

Try to include the discussion strategies and the patterns from the personalization section in the following discussions.

Do you think income tax should be increased or reduced? Why?
Do you think consumption tax should be increased or reduced? Why?
What other taxes should be increased or reduced? Why?
How can the government encourage consumption to increase?
Do you think unemployment is an unfortunate necessity? Why?
What effects does inflation have on exports and imports and on society as a whole?
If you were in charge of your country's economy, what would you do?

Activities

FOLLOW-UP QUESTIONS

List three ways of increasing business productivity in your country.

Example: Companies should use computers more.

Now talk to another student and ask at least two follow-up questions about each point.

Examples:

A: Surely most companies already use computers a lot?

B: Maybe, but they don't use them efficiently enough. Computers can lead to great increases in productivity.

A: Does that mean people will lose their jobs?

B   Not if they learn to use computers. It only means that each person will be able to produce more in the same time.

ROLE PLAY

Student A:	*You are a successful businessman/ woman.*
Student B:	*Interview A and ask him/her what makes a good businessman/ woman.*

Example questions:

What qualities should a good businessman or woman have?

Why is honesty so important?

SITUATION - STARTING A BUSINESS

Work in pairs, groups, or as a whole class.

(1)   *Decide on a business you would like to start, and then work out how to set it up. Consider factors such as where to get capital, the location of the business, the marketing strategy, etc., and make a business forecast for the first one or two years.*

Examples:

Why don't we start a publishing company?

We could try to get a loan from the bank.

We'd have to employ reps to visit all the bookstores.

What kind of books do you think we should publish?

How are we going to find people to write the books?

We could always write them ourselves.

(2)   *Design publicity material for your new business, and plan how to use it.*

Examples:

I think we should make a catalogue of all our books.

Perhaps the layout could be something like this.

I think it needs more photographs.

It would be expensive to make it as big as that.

What kind of logo do you think we should have?

What colors do you think we should use?

"People say I'm very successful. But success is relative. The more successful I become, the more relatives I seem to have."

13. Economics

Further Activities

COLLOCATION SETS

Put the following into sentences or dialogues.

Economy

1. booming economy   *Example:*   The economy was booming for a few years, but now it's in recession.

2. revive the economy
3. a false economy

Business

1. business relationship   *Example:*   My company has an important business relationship with an internet company.

2. business objective
3. mix business with pleasure

Tax

1. tax rebate   *Example:*   I got a tax rebate this month, so I'm going to treat myself to a big dinner.

2. deduct tax
3. a tax cut

SPEECHES

Prepare a short speech on one of these three topics.

The government and businesses should work closely together.
Weaker companies should be taken over by larger and stronger companies.
If we say we believe in market forces, we mean we believe in the law of the jungle.

EXTRA EXPRESSIONS

Put the following into short dialogues.

take time off   business as usual
The end justifies the means.   get ... money's worth

Example:
A: I know we'll have to lay off a few hundred people, but it will make the company profitable again.
B: The end doesn't always justify the means.

"I'm self-employed and can never take time off work."
"Because your office couldn't manage if you weren't there?"
"No, because they could manage very well. And I don't want them to find out."

Consolidation & Recycling

BUILDING VOCABULARY

Across

1 Reducing advertising will be a ___ economy.
3 The last election ___ was very close.
7 Some people want power for its own ___.
8 We need to boost exports to reduce the trade ___.
10 Rising prices.
12 The end justifies the ___.
14 I'm a law–___ citizen.
15 ___'s just talk.
18 Teachers just want us to ___ to what they say.
20 I must set a good ___.
23 Business is good. We're making a ___.
24 Our business is ___ the rocks.
25 We live in a male–___ society.
26 There's no difference in the murder ___.

Down

1 ___ of the press.
2 Not moving.
4 Supply ___ demand.
5 A being from another planet.
6 A member of the UN.
9 I'm surrounded by sexual ___ at work.
11 Politicians seem so different from ___ people.
13 Governments should give more ___ to developing countries.
16 There should be two main political ___.
17 What are the current economic ___ in your country?
19 The long-term ___ should be very positive.
21 Money is the ___ cause of selfishness.
22 I have to pay back my student ___.

FOCUSING ON COLLOCATIONS

Write eight separate sentences, each of which includes both words in the pairs below.

long-term / effect
foreign / policy
business / pleasure
quick / thinking

trade / deficit
hit / off
spoil / view
revive / economy

WRITING OPINIONS

Write paragraphs about the following. Try to include words and patterns from this unit.

Tax.
How my country's economy should be improved.
A business I'd like to start.

REFLECTION

Which section of the unit did you find most interesting?
In which section of the unit did you learn the most?
Make a list of any new words and patterns from this unit that you want to try and remember.
You may find it helpful to write each word or pattern on a card.

14. Happiness

WARM-UP QUESTIONS

When do you feel the happiest?
When you have problems, can you look on the bright side of things?
How could your life become much happier?
What do you think your answers tell you about yourself?

VOCABULARY

Here are some words and expressions that will be useful in this unit.
How many do you know?

calm	mood	inhibited
make the best of	fulfilling	sense of achievement
satisfied	make the most of	complain
miss out on	goal	think positively

Discuss which of the above words and expressions could fit in the following gaps.

Chen: I don't know if I'm happy or not. I certainly try to ____ the opportunities that come my way, but I don't really have a clear ____ in life and don't go looking for opportunities. I guess I'm too ____, so I ____ a lot of things. How about you? Are you happy?

Abena: Well, I find it easy to stay ____, and I'm usually in a good ____, so I guess I'm reasonably happy. When it comes down to it, I don't have a lot to ____ about. However, I don't feel deeply ____ by anything I do. I'm still looking for something ____.

Chen: Speaking very frankly, my job's boring, I can't find a girlfriend, and I don't have much money, but I ____ my situation and try to ____. I always tell myself that things can only get better.

What words and expressions that are not in the list can you think of that might be useful when talking about happiness?

MIND MAP

Here is Chen's mind map starting from 'Am I happy?'

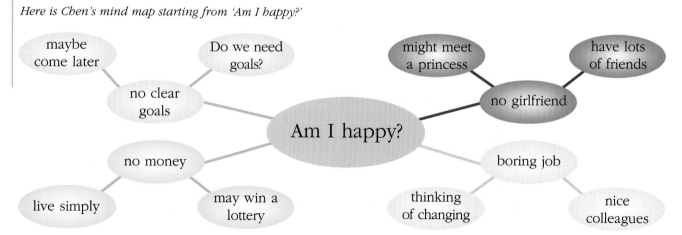

Now make your own mind map with 'Am I happy?', 'my goals', 'a happy person', or 'making the best of things' in the center. Talk about your mind map with another student or the rest of the class.

Always – Universal, ph: Gary Graver

POINTS OF VIEW - I WISH I COULD HAVE A GOOD TIME

I wish I could live forever on a romantic Pacific island. I'd lie on the beach, eat exotic food, dance all night ... That's my idea of happiness. I can think of nothing better than to be surrounded by beautiful things and having a good time.

I don't think I'd be satisfied by that. It'd be great for a while, but I'd feel I was wasting my life. I need more purpose or direction. I need to feel I'm creating or improving things. Just satisfying my senses isn't enough. The kind of satisfaction you're talking about doesn't last very long.

You could paint beautiful pictures, build a dream house, raise a happy family ... There are so many different ways of finding happiness on a paradise island. You don't have to sit in an office in order to find a purpose in life.

I know that's true, and I respect all those ways of living, but to me they're not wide enough. They're all concerned with the immediate world around us. I want to do something to improve society as a whole, however small it may be. That's what makes me happy.

Unit 14: Happiness • 87

14. Happiness

Practice and Discussion

PERSONALIZATION

Complete these sentences with your own ideas.

My idea of happiness is to …
I can think of nothing better than …
I'd like to be surrounded by …
I don't think I'd be satisfied by …
I need/don't need to work to …
… is one way of finding happiness.
To me … is/are not … enough.
I want to do something to …

I'd like to be surrounded by beautiful works of art.

"My son dreams of being a magician. He never stops thinking about pulling rabbits out of hats, sawing people in half and that kind of thing."
"Is he your only child?"
"No, he has a number of half brothers and half sisters."

DISCUSSION

This apartment's OK for the time being, but I'm looking for somewhere nicer.

DISCUSSION STRATEGIES

… for a while, but …
… for the time being, but …
… n't last (very) long.

Try to include the discussion strategies and the patterns from the personalization section in the following discussions.

Are happiness and having a good time the same thing?
What brings lasting happiness?
Do you need to be doing things for society to be happy?
What do you think you could do to help society as a whole?
Do you have a purpose in life? If so, talk about it. If not, how do you think you may find it?
When do you feel creative?
How do you deal with unhappiness?

Activities

FOLLOW-UP QUESTIONS

List three things that make you unhappy.

Example: Paying the rent.

Now talk to another student and ask at least two follow-up questions about each point.

Examples:

A: Are you very short of money?

B: Not really, but my rent's too high.

A: Why not move to a different place?

B: No, I like where I'm living. It's just too expensive. And I always feel depressed when the time to pay the rent is approaching.

ROLE PLAY

Student A: *Play the role of a Hollywood star. You have a lot of problems.*

Examples:

You are becoming less popular, have to work more than one day a week, have lost your photograph album, haven't been to a party for a week, don't have enough servants.

Student B: *Show Student A that each of his/her problems has a positive side to it.*

Examples:

Trying to become popular again will be a new challenge.

If you work more, it'll stop you from getting bored.

SITUATION - COMPLAINING

Brainstorming: *Think of things in your daily life that annoy you.*
Think of ways of coming to terms with each of these things.
Think of both gentle and direct ways to complain about each of these things.

Student A: *Be yourself. Complain about all the things you don't like - at home, at school, at work.*
Argue with Student B.

Examples:

My teacher always gets impatient with me!

I have too much work to do.

My boss always tells bad jokes and expects me to laugh.

Student B: *Argue with Student A.*

Examples:

Perhaps you should do your work more quickly.

It might be worse if he was always serious.

It's normal for people doing your kind of job to wear a tie.

"I gave you a film two weeks ago! What's taking so long?!"
"I'm afraid we can't find your photographs, madam."
"Oh well, never mind. One day my prints will come."

14. Happiness

Further Activities

COLLOCATION SETS

Put the following into sentences or dialogues.

Happy
1. happy together
2. happy memory
3. happy ending

Example: They are just right for each other. They look so happy together.

Mood
1. in the mood
2. a playful mood
3. a generous mood

Example: She wants me to play tennis, but I'm not in the mood right now.

Satisfied
1. completely satisfied

Example: I was disappointed that she turned up so late but completely satisfied by her explanation.

2. self-satisfied
3. a satisfied customer/client

SPEECHES

Prepare a short speech on one of these three topics.

Real happiness comes from helping others.
Success doesn't bring happiness.
Only children are really happy.

EXTRA EXPRESSIONS

Put the following into short dialogues.

mixed feelings   blissfully happy
A change is as good as a rest.   for a change

Example:
A: I have mixed feelings about leaving.
B: I know what you mean. I know it's time to move on, but I really love this place.

"For twenty years my wife and I were blissfully happy, and then we met."

Consolidation & Recycling

BUILDING VOCABULARY

Across

1. One person.
6. Layers of seniority.
8. I'm in a good ___ today.
9. Employer or manager.
10. I was in an absurd ___.
11. It has ___ to do with me.
12. You'll ___ out on a lot of fun.
14. There's evidence to ___ that TV affects crime.
17. There was a sudden ___ of violence.
19. We were able to ___ out of court.
20. Freedom of ___.
21. More men should ___ ___ housework.

Down

1. Reserved or hesitant.
2. Without responsibility.
3. Decreasing.
4. I like a story with a happy ___.
5. Somebody left wing.
7. The earth is in a ___ part of the universe.
13. Many patients ___ from side effects.
15. The ___ of war may be an effective deterrrent.
16. Your ___ is as good as mine.
18. The human ___ may not survive much longer.

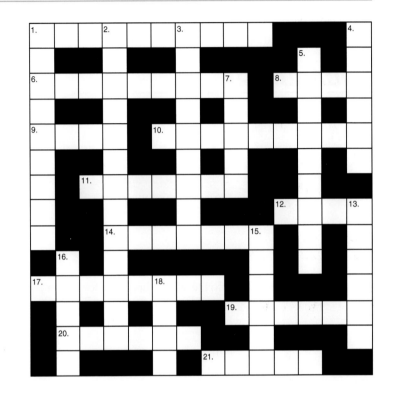

FOCUSING ON COLLOCATIONS

Write eight separate sentences, each of which includes both words in the pairs below.

in / mood   happy / memory
tax / rebate   take / credit
miss / out   own / sake
emergency / aid   mixed / feelings

WRITING OPINIONS

Write paragraphs about the following. Try to include words and patterns from this unit.

Making the most of opportunities.
My happiest memories.
How to live happily ever after.

REFLECTION

Which section of the unit did you find most interesting?
In which section of the unit did you learn the most?
Make a list of any new words and patterns from this unit that you want to try and remember.
You may find it helpful to write each word or pattern on a card.

15. Globalization

WARM-UP QUESTIONS

Talk about friends you have had from other countries.
Talk about other countries you have visited.
Can you easily forget that somebody you are talking with is from a different country or of a different race?
What do you think your answers tell you about yourself?

VOCABULARY

Here are some words and expressions that will be useful in this unit. How many do you know?

melting pots	stereotypes	cosmopolitan
open-minded	homogeneous	perspectives
global	outlook	ethnic minorities
backgrounds	multi-racial	heterogeneous

Discuss which of the above words and expressions could fit in the following gaps.

Abena: Exposure to the world through information provided by the ____ media may be leading to the false impression that more people are developing an international ____, whereas, in fact, it may be making many people less ____.

Nazim: I can see that members of ____ may feel their cultures are being suppressed by standardized ____ ____. This may be particularly true in ____ areas rather than ____ ones. In the larger cities, I think people have more ____ ways of thinking.

Abena: I'm not convinced that the larger ____ cities are the ____ they are supposed to be. Things may be worse when people from different racial and ethnic ____ live side by side. Even the most well-informed experts in these apparently ____ cities often express opinions that seem to be based on prejudice and ____.

What words and expressions that are not in the list can you think of that might be useful when talking about globalization?

MIND MAP

Here is Abena's mind map starting from 'international attitudes'.

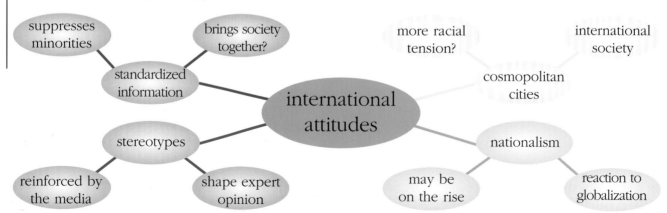

Now make your own mind map with 'international attitudes', 'ethnic minorities', 'cosmopolitan cities', or 'learning to be international' in the center. Talk about your mind map with another student or the rest of the class.

POINTS OF VIEW - LEARNING ABOUT THE WORLD MAKES US INTERNATIONAL

The enthusiastic way my teachers taught me about life in other countries stimulated my interest in seeing the world for myself, and I've had itchy feet ever since. If I hadn't traveled so much, I'd probably still have a nationalistic view of the world. I'm very grateful to those teachers who got me interested in the world in the first place.

I wonder if it's as straightforward as that. When I visit other countries, I often run into people who have never been abroad, are not well educated, and yet seem to be able to accept different ways of thinking easily. On the other hand, I meet people from the same countries who have traveled and have more knowledge of the world, but who come across as being very uninternational.

I guess a lot of people don't take advantage of the opportunities they have at school, or when they travel. But I still believe educating students about the world is the key to making our society more international.

I think it goes deeper than that. I think we are born with flexible and curious minds, and the education system, with its focus on knowledge and facts, dampens this down. Many of us would be more international if we didn't succeed at school, or if we were given more training in questioning fundamentals and looking at things from many points of view. We could then reach our potential as full members of the international community.

15. Globalization

Practice and Discussion

PERSONALIZATION

Complete these sentences with your own ideas.

If I hadn't … I would still …
I'm very grateful to …
I often run into people who …
… come(s) across as …
I don't take enough advantage of …
… is/are the key to …
People are born with …
We can reach more of our potential by …

> *I often run into people who I vaguely remember from a long time ago.*

"I'm glad I wasn't born in China!"
"Why's that?"
"I can't speak a word of Chinese."

DISCUSSION

> *They say oily food causes heart problems, but I wonder if it's as clear cut as that.*

DISCUSSION STRATEGIES

I wonder if it's as straightforward as that.
It goes deeper than that.
I wonder if it's as clear cut as that.

Try to include the discussion strategies and the patterns from the personalization section in the following discussions.

Are we born with naturally curious and flexible minds?
What effect does the way we are educated and brought up have on this?
Can we educate children to have international minds? If so, how?
How has the way you have been brought up influenced your view of the world?
What can we do by ourselves to become more international?
What needs to change if we are to have a truly international and peaceful world?
What is an international person?

Activities

STEREOTYPES

(1)   *List the first thoughts that come into your head when you think of these countries:*
The USA, France, China, Britain, Egypt, India, Germany.

Talk about whether these associations are reasonable or not.

Example:
Britain - fog and rain

A: I stayed in Britain for a month, and I never saw any fog. It didn't rain very much, either, though British people complained that it usually does.

(2)   *Do the same for the character of people living in these countries.*

Example:
French people - they don't like to speak English.

A: When I visited France, I never had any trouble when I spoke English, though that might have been because I spent most of the time with young people.

SITUATION - GIVING A GUIDED TOUR

Brainstorming: *Think of local customs in your country.*
Think of the popular image of your country.
Think of how much of this image is true or false.

Student A: *You are a visitor from another country. Interview Student B about the culture and customs of his/her country.*

Examples:
What are the popular festivals?
Tell me about some of the traditional food. Why do you
    think people originally ate ... ?
What do you think is the origin of ... ?

Student B: *Be yourself.*

Examples:
I think it has something to do with the climate.
People from other countries often say we are very
    warm-hearted.
I think it was originally a harvest festival.

"The traditional dancing in your country is so energetic!"
"It isn't usually. The waiter just dropped some ice cubes down her back."

15. Globalization

Further Activities

COLLOCATION SETS

Put the following into sentences or dialogues.

International

1. an international conference   *Example:*   There'll be an international conference on the environment in London next month.

2. an international reputation
3. The International Monetary Fund (IMF)

World

1. see the world   *Example:*   I'm fed up with staying in one place. I want to see the world.
2. world opinion
3. in a perfect world

Global

1. global coverage   *Example:*   The murder in my home town received global news coverage.
2. global economy
3. global ban

SPEECHES

Prepare a short speech on one of these three topics.

The development of TV and computers has been bringing the world together in a positive way.

It's important to be proud of one's country.

Having native speakers as assistants in a foreign language class often doesn't help students become more international.

EXTRA EXPRESSIONS

Put the following into short dialogues.

It takes all sorts to make a world.
put yourself in ... shoes/place

from place to place
... world is falling apart

Example:

A: I can't understand why you got angry.
B: Try putting yourself in my shoes!
      How would you feel if I did that to you?

"It's interesting how customs vary from country to country. For example, in my country, most people stir their coffee with their left hand."
"That's interesting. In my country, we usually use a spoon."

Consolidation & Recycling

BUILDING VOCABULARY

Across
1. I'm not ___ that large cities are cosmopolitan.
7. ___ minorities.
9. A sweeping ___.
10. That will always ___ a mystery.
11. A ___ pot.
13. They can't provide free health care ___ more.
16. The tip of the ___.
18. It comes ___ as insincere.
19. ___ business with pleasure.
20. Much of our ___ to the world is through standardized information.
22. The ducks are far away from their natural ___.
25. It takes all ___ to make a world.
26. There's no money left. We've been making ___ for two years.

Down
1. If taxes are reduced, ___ will increase.
2. With some ___ exceptions.
3. The ___ effect could be tragic.
4. I'm about as pessimistic as they ___.
5. We may permanently ___ the ecosystem.
6. He was just an innocent ___.
8. It will do more ___ than good.
12. You should ___ if you have a sore throat.
14. We compared the Gross National ___ of all countries.
15. The police have questioned many ___.
17. Look on the ___ side.
18. The government is making an ___ for aid.
21. I pay ___ much tax!
23. Everybody seems to see me ___ a positive person.
24. I'm not sure what ___ do with it.

FOCUSING ON COLLOCATIONS

Write eight separate sentences, each of which includes both words in the pairs below.

global / coverage   make / most
make / best   end / means
ethnic / background   become / complacent
settle / court   starting / capital

WRITING OPINIONS

Write paragraphs about the following. Try to include words and patterns from this unit.

The United Nations.
The dangers of terrorism.
The future of the world.

REFLECTION

Which section of the unit did you find most interesting?
In which section of the unit did you learn the most?
Make a list of any new words and patterns from this unit that you want to try and remember.
You may find it helpful to write each word or pattern on a card.

Featured Movies

Made in America *(pg 8)*
(1993) Warner Bros
Ted Danson, Whoopi Goldberg, Nia Long
Director: Richard Benjamin

Sarah Matthews runs a bookstore, and she is raising her college-age daughter, Zora, alone. Hal Jackson is a car dealer and the biggest fool in town. Imagine Zora's surprise when she discovers accidentally that she is the product of artificial insemination, and, due to a mistake at the clinic, her father is Hal! He's not too happy either – a committed bachelor with no interest in starting or raising a family.

The Bourne Identity *(pg 14)*
(2002) Hypnotic/Universal
Matt Damon, Franka Potente
Director: Doug Liman

A wounded man is discovered by fishermen who nurse him back to health. He remembers nothing but starts rebuilding his memory based on a Swiss bank account, the number of which is implanted in his hip. He realizes that he is being hunted and takes off with Marie, his new lover, on a search to find out who he is and why he is being hunted.

At the Circus *(pg 20)*
(1939) MGM
Groucho Marx, Chico Marx, Harpo Marx
Director: Edward Buzzell

The owner of a small circus owes money to his partner. Before he can pay, his partner steals the money so that he can take over the circus. Enter the circus strongman's assistant Punchy (Harpo) and friend (Chico) who enlist the help of dubious lawyer J. Cheever Loophole (Groucho) to get the money back. With one hilarious gag following another, this is another classic Marx Brothers comedy caper – featuring a gorilla named Gibraltar!

Dead Poets Society *(pg 26)*
(1989) Touchstone Pictures
Robin Williams, Ethan Hawke
Director: Peter Weir

Shy Todd Anderson (Hawke) has been sent to the school where his popular older brother was valedictorian. His roommate, Neil, although bright and popular, is very much under the thumb of his overbearing father. The two, along with their other friends, meet Professor Keating (Williams), their new English teacher, who tells them of the Dead Poets Society and encourages them to go against the status quo. Each of them does this, and their lives change from the experience.

Keystone Cops *(pg 32)*
Sennett Films

Mack Sennett was the director who popularized slapstick on the big screen and created American institutions such as the Keystone Cops. His Keystone films (1912-1933) were short, action-packed comedies that featured fantastic Keystone Cops chases, frequent tossing of custard cream pies, and scenes with scantily-clad barelegged women (known as the Sennett bathing beauties). To this day, the Keystone films are admired as early masterpieces of comic movie-making.

Sound of Music *(pg 38)*
(1965) 20th Century Fox
Julie Andrews, Christopher Plummer
Director: Robert Wise

Maria had always wanted to be a nun, but when she became old enough to enter a convent, she discovered it wasn't what she thought it would be. Often in trouble, Maria is sent to the house of widowed Captain Von Trapp to care for his seven rowdy children. The children have scared off countless governesses, but Maria perseveres and soon learns that all these children need is a little love. Maria teaches them to sing, bringing music back into the hearts and home of the Von Trapp family.

Independence Day *(pg 44)*
(1996) 20th Century Fox
Will Smith, Bill Pullman, Jeff Goldblum
Director: Roland Emmerich

Independence Day is a pastiche of flying-saucer movies from the 1940s and 1950s. The ultimate encounter begins when mysterious and powerful aliens launch an all out invasion against the human race. One morning, massive spaceships appear in Earth's skies, but amazement soon turns to terror as the ships destroy major cities worldwide. The world's only hope lies with a determined band of survivors who unite for one last strike against the extraterrestrial invaders.

Waterloo *(pg 50)*
(1970) De Laurentiis/Mosfilm
Rod Steiger, Christopher Plummer, Orson Welles
Director: Sergei Bondarchuk

After defeating France and imprisoning Napoleon on Elba, Europe is shocked to find Napoleon has escaped, and the French Army has rallied around him. Arthur Wellesley, Duke of Wellington, is the best British general, but he has never faced Napoleon. Wellesley confronts Napoleon with a mixed army of Prussians, mercenaries, British, and Belgians. A victory for Napoleon would plunge Europe back into a long-term war. The two armies meet at Waterloo where the fate of Europe is decided ...

Erin Brockovich *(pg 56)*
(2000) Universal
Julia Roberts, Albert Finney, Aaron Eckhart
Director: Steven Soderbergh

Broke and desperate, twice-divorced single mom Erin forces her way into a clerical job with attorney Ed Masry. A suspicious connection between industrial waste from a local power company and the poisoned water supply of a small local town comes to her attention, and she makes winning justice and compensation for the townsfolk her personal mission. Based upon a true story, Erin Brockovich proves that greed, neglect, and corporate arrogance can be overcome.

Out of Africa *(pg 62)*
(1985) Universal
Meryl Streep, Robert Redford
Director: Sydney Pollack

Sydney Pollack's 1985 multiple-Oscar® winner is a powerful film about the life of Karen Blixen (Streep), a Danish baroness. She travels to Kenya with her husband, and they start a coffee plantation. She slowly adjusts to her new environment, but her married life begins to unravel when her husband disappears on long trips. While the acting is excellent, the real star of the film is the African landscape - beautiful images that provide the perfect backdrop to the human romances that play out on screen.

Ali *(pg 68)*
(2001) Columbia
Will Smith, Jon Voight, Jamie Foxx
Director: Michael Mann

Bold and outspoken, Cassius Clay is an entirely new kind of African-American sportsman. Proud and self-confident, he knows he can be the greatest boxer of all time. He soon claims the heavyweight championship, but his personal life is controversial with his allegiance to the Nation of Islam, his friendship with Malcolm X, and his abandonment of his birth name in favor of Muhammad Ali. Many of his greatest battles were to be fought outside the ring.

The American President *(pg 74)*
(1995) Castle Rock/Universal/Wildwood
Michael Douglas, Annette Bening, Martin Sheen
Director: Rob Reiner

Andrew Shepherd (Douglas) is President of the United States and a lonely single parent. After three years in office, he starts thinking about the possibility of dating. His first encounter is with cut-throat environmental lobbyist Sydney Ellen Wade (Bening). Sparks begin to crackle, and the two begin a tentative, turbulent, but heartfelt romance.

Rogue Trader *(pg 80)*
(1999) Granada Film Productions
Ewan McGregor, Anna Friel
Director: James Dearden

Ambitious but inexperienced Nick Leeson (McGregor) has been promoted to run the trading operation for an international bank in Singapore. Unsupervised and free to invest as he wishes, he begins to lose control and recklessly gambles investors' money. Before long, a complete financial meltdown looms, his employer faces bankruptcy, and Leeson himself faces criminal action for breaking several financial laws.

Always *(pg 86)*
(1989) Universal
Richard Dreyfuss, Holly Hunter, Audrey Hepburn
Director: Steven Spielberg

Pete Sandich (Dreyfuss) is a daredevil fire-fighting pilot, putting out forest fires by dropping water on them. After promising his frightened fiancée Dorinda (Hunter) to finally keep his feet on the ground, Pete is killed during one last flight. His spirit wanders restlessly, attached to and protective of the woman he loves, but when a likeable trainee pilot begins wooing Dorinda, it becomes Pete's heavenly responsibility to assist in their budding romance and help her find happiness. Audrey Hepburn makes her final screen appearance as an angel.

Casino Royale *(pg 92)*
(1967) Columbia
David Niven, Peter Sellers, Ursula Andress, Woody Allen
Directors: Val Guest, John Huston, and others

In this 1967 all-star spoof of Ian Fleming's 007 agent, the aging Sir James Bond (Niven) is called out of retirement to take on the organized threat of SMERSH. Enemy agents attempt to compromise him, and his job is made difficult by his idiot son, Jimmy Bond (Allen), but, true to form, Bond is unflappable and ever the gentleman.

Patterns & Collocation*

THE FOLLOWING IS A SELECTION OF PATTERNS AND COLLOCATIONS FROM THE COURSE.

They set a bad example, especially to children. 69
It's not as bad as all that. 39

Bail
If I become President, I'll stop bailing out the airlines. 77

Barrier
If every country ... reduced import barriers ... .63

Based
... seem to be based on prejudice 92

Basic
Health care is a basic human right. 21

Basis
... that's still the basis of modern European law. .51

Become
What's the best way to become a millionaire? . .17
Have you considered studying to become a nurse? 29
Do they dream of becoming President some day? .74
Patients might become very sick or die unnecessarily. 23
The more successful I become, the more 83
They often become complacent. 75

Being
... to assume we are the only intelligent beings. 45
This apartment's OK for the time being, but ... 88

Better
I think it'd be better if I marry somebody who's 9
... like to take better care of your health 20
Shouldn't society be setting a better example? .33
Won't somebody make me a better offer? 17
Do you feel financially better off or worse off than ... ? 80
I can think of nothing better than to be 87
At least things are better than they used to be. 57
Things can only get better. 86
Something's better than nothing. 66

Birth
... should first focus on birth control programs. 62

Blood
... and shoot them in cold blood. 68

Boost
... and boost consumption so as to stimulate ... 80
... and boost productivity so as to stimulate ... .80

They should boost spending. 80
It will give the economy a boost. 81

Born
... think that way from the moment they are born. .57
For most of it I wasn't even born. 58

Break
Think of rules a student might break. 29
Would you ever break the law? 34
How did you break your leg? 47
War may break out very soon. 54

Bright
What do you think that bright light is? 48
Let's look on the bright side. 12

Business
Make a business forecast for the first one or two
  years. 83
... an important business relationship with 84
We need to be clear about our business objectives. 84
My new business is now secure. 82
... is a good way to mix business with pleasure. .84
It's business as usual. 84
Mind your own business! 72

Calm
Well, I find it easy to stay calm. 86
Calm down! 72

Cancer
Many people will die of cancer caused by ... .39
Pesticides may cause cancer. 41

Capital
I could use my savings as starting capital. 14
... more capital to invest in building factories ... 63

Care / careful
I think medical care should be free for everybody. 21
Health care is a basic human right. 21
How do you take care of your health? 20
A doctor should care about all patients equally. 23
... genuinely care about ordinary people. 77
Don't you care if you fail your exams? 29
I couldn't care less. 12
We just have to be more careful. 39
If I'm not careful I could easily get a rash 20

Patterns & Collocation

Case
Think of ways a teacher can help in each case. 29
In a recent court case 36

Caught
... constantly caught up in wars. 50

Cause
Think of problems that cause stress. 11
Pesticides may cause cancer. 41
What do you think the causes of these changes are? 38
... cancer caused by too much ultra-violet radiation. 39
The immediate effect of ... might be to cause inflation ... 81

Center
Do you like to be the center of attention? 8
Lessons tended to be student-centered. 26
The lessons are so teacher-centered! 30
... small elites of self-centered, ambitious politicians. 78

Certainly
I certainly try to make the most of the opportunities 86

Charity
We can give part of our income to charity. . . .65
I'm very careful about which charities I donate
    money to. 65
All the proceeds from ... will go to charity. . . .66

Cheer
He always tries to cheer me up. 59

Chemical
We have to stop using toxic chemicals. 38

Civil
When doctors are civil servants, they don't ... .21
... or in some civil war. 50

Class
She's in a class of her own. 30

Clear
I don't have clear goals. 8
... needs to have clearer foreign policy objectives. .78
... some great medicine that will clear everything up. 20
They say ..., but I wonder if it's as clear cut as that. 94

Close
... close down all nuclear power plants. 41

Come
I'm about as narrow-minded as they come. . . .8
At the end of the day, it all comes down to money. 28
I came across so much racial prejudice. 12
... but even ... come across as insincere. 74
... the opportunities that come my way. 86
When it comes down to it, I don't have 86
... ways of coming to terms with each of 89
I don't know if/whether I'm coming or going. .12

Completely
He would never completely understand me. . . .9
The weather is completely different from 38
... discover some completely new technology. .44
... but completely satisfied by her explanation. 90

Complicated
It's not as complicated as that. 16

Compulsory
All subjects were compulsory until 26

Concerned
They're all concerned with the ... world around us. 87

Conclusion
We mustn't jump to conclusions. 36

Conditioned
They are conditioned to think that way. 57

Confidence
The Prime Minister may lose a vote of no confidence. 78

Connection
I had no connection with the crime at all. 32

Consider / consideration
Have you considered studying to become a nurse? .29
... consider the consequences of their actions. .33
Consider factors such as where to get capital ... 83
A far more important consideration is that if ... 33

Consumed
Even ... come across as consumed by ambition. 74

Patterns & Collocation

Ear

It went in one ear and out the other. 24

Earn

Why don't they get jobs and earn money to ... ?17
I might earn a lot. 14
It's very hard to earn a living these days. 18
It wouldn't earn much interest. 14

Easy / easily

If I'm not careful, I could easily get a rash ... .20
Can women easily become political leaders? . . .76
Can you easily forget that somebody you are ... ? .92
It makes it easier for the wealthier countries to ... 63
Well, I find it easy to stay calm. 86
That's easy to say! I have a son to support! . . .64

Economic

The President's economic policy seems to be ... 78
What are the current economic trends ... ? 80
... economic problems the world is facing? 80
Economic growth is stagnating. 80
The global economic situation. 80

Economy

... the world economy would grow 63
... you want the western economies and Japan to ... 63
... benefits local people and the local economy. 65
The long-term effects would benefit the economy. 81
... doing its best to revive the economy. 84
This makes the economy less dynamic. 21
The economy was booming for a few years. . .84
The economy is in recession. 84
It will give the economy a boost. 81
The economy's in a mess. 80
It would be a false economy to cut 85
Their economies cannot grow. 62
... reducing ... and revitalizing their economies. 62

Ecosystem

... permanently destroyed the Earth's ecosystem. 38
The world's ecosystem will be permanently damaged. 39

Effect

What are the positive and negative effects of ... ? .22
The immediate effect of ... might be to 81
The long-term effects would benefit the economy. 81
... caused by the greenhouse effect. 38

Election

Then hold an election. 77
As far as we could tell, the election was fair. . .78
It was obvious the election had been rigged. .78
There would be an election every four or five years. 75
To win a majority in an election, he or she has to ... .74

Emissions

Even if we cut down on carbon dioxide emissions. 38

Enable

... that enables us to travel through black holes. 44

Encourage

We need competition to encourage us to 15
They should encourage exports. 80
We need to encourage innovation. 80

End

I suppose everything turned out OK in the end. 32
At the end of the day, it all comes down to money. .28
... was touch and go until the very end. 78
I'm sure there'll be a happy ending. 90
The end justifies the means. 84

Entice

There was nothing to entice us to study for ourselves. 26

Entitled

Everybody over eighteen is entitled to vote. . .78

Environment / environmental

... can we do to improve the environment? . . .38
All countries need to ... for protecting the environment. 39
Detergents harm the environment. 42
If we don't adapt to the environment, we 42
Is your local environment improving ... ? 40
... a more international environment. 9
Environmental problems. 38
You are an environmental activist trying to ... .41

Equal / equally

People talk about equal opportunities. 56
We're supposed to be equal to men. 57
Men and women should be treated equally. . .56

Escalating

The amount of violence is escalating. 72

Patterns & Collocation

Patterns & Collocation

Go

Good

Goods

Government

Gross

Grow

Guarantee

Guess

Half

Hand

Happen

Happy / happiness

Harm / harmful

Head

Health

Heavy

Help

I can't help the way I feel. 9
... who really need help have to wait longer ... 21
... others will care or try to help if a man cries. 59
Every little bit helps. 66
... before expecting help from rich countries. .66

Hesitation

... that you trust people without hesitation. 8

History

What lessons can we learn from history? 52
School textbook writers are trying to rewrite history. 54
... Revolution changed the course of history. . .54
History often repeats itself. 54

Hit

Why did you hit him so hard? 35
Then I hit on a good idea. 72
That's exactly right! You hit the nail on the head! . .72
I knew we were going to hit it off. 72

Home

... who reminds you of an alien from back home. 47
We will build more retirement homes for old people. 77
... in my home town received global news coverage. 96
A woman's place is in the home. 60

Honeymoon

At first there was a honeymoon period when ... 54

Human

... cause of selfishness in human relationships. 15
Health care is a basic human right. 21
It's human nature. 15
... says that human beings sometimes 33
The human race may not survive much longer. 39

Ice

The polar ice caps will melt. 39
I'm afraid it's just the tip of the iceberg. 42
... just dropped some ice cubes down her back. 95

Idea

Then I hit on a good idea. 72
Your idea is ... not inspiring enough. 75
... the need for new, progressive ideas 80
That's my idea of happiness. 87

Illusion

That way of thinking is just an illusion. 57

Image

Think of the popular image of your country. . .95
Think of how much of this image is true or false. 95

Imagined / imaginary

I've always imagined that you trust people. . . .8
... any of my boyfriend's flirting – real or imagined! . .8
... your girlfriend/boyfriend (real or imaginary). 59

Immediate / immediately

Violent crime increases immediately after a ... .69
The immediate effect of a reduction in income tax ... 81
... concerned with the immediate world around us. 87

Import

If every country in the world reduced import barriers ... 63

Impression

... leading to the false impression that more ... 92

Improve

... could develop and improve your attitudes? . .10
I would improve my life. 14
... to continually develop and improve society. 15
... can we do to improve the environment? . . .38
How would you improve the country's economy? .77
... and improve health care at the same time? . .77

Increase

The crime rate continues to increase. 36
The money supply should be increased. 80
Investment should be increased. 80
... taxes are reduced, consumption will increase. 81
Production will increase too 81
Demand for goods increases, so 81
The value of the shares will increase. 14
There is pressure to increase pay. 81
Computers can lead to great increases in productivity. 83

Indicate

Market research ... indicates that there's no ... .80

Industrial / industrializing

It wasn't until the Industrial Revolution that 50
... in factories in the industrializing countries. .50

Patterns & Collocation

Informed
Even the most well-informed experts 92

Ingredients
All the food here contains natural ingredients. .42

Innovation
It was a time of artistic innovation. 50
We need to encourage innovation. 80

Interest
He's lost interest in everything. 16
... why interest groups have so much influence. 74
... stimulated my interest in seeing the world ... 93
It wouldn't earn much interest. 14
The interest is low. 14

International
... a more international environment. 9
... somebody considering an international marriage? 10
... should be paid to an international organization. 39
... developing an international outlook. 92
... as full members of the international community. 93
Can we educate children to have international minds? .94
... is developing an international reputation as a ... .96
The International Monetary Fund (IMF) is insisting ... 96

Into
... go into your marriage with a positive attitude ... 9
... just rub it into your stiff muscles 20
The Police are looking into it. 36
I often run into people who have never 93

Invest
... the best ways to save or invest money? 16
... have more capital to invest in building factories ... 63

Involved
They get so involved in politics 77

Issue
... compromises on most contentious issues. . .75
... other special issues you want to mention. . .77

Itchy
I've had itchy feet ever since. 93

Just
It's unfair to ban physical sports just because the ... 69

... been just as aggressive as male leaders. . . .51
He wasn't just a great general. 51
We'll just have to accept that our ways of thinking ... 12
Government health care just doesn't work! 21
... but it's just talk. 80
They are just right for each other. 90
I realised that way of thinking is just an illusion ... 57
It's just a matter of time. 54
I'm afraid it's just the tip of the iceberg. 42

Knowledge
Doctors didn't have enough medical knowledge ... 53
... have more knowledge of the world. 93

Large
Why should we spend large amounts of money ... ? .33
... a campaign that requires large sums of money. 74

Last / lasting
I only resort to violence as a last resort. 72
We didn't know ... until the last minute. 78
The kind of satisfaction ... doesn't last very long. .87
What brings lasting happiness? 88

Lateral.
She's good at lateral thinking. 12

Law
... between 'against the law' and 'illegal'? 34
Would you ever break the law? 34
Even criminals with families should obey the law. 35
Most of us live peaceful, law-abiding lives. . .68
We mean we believe in the law of the jungle. .84

Lay
I know we'll have to lay off a few hundred people. 84

Layer
... problems like the thinning of the ozone layer. .39

Learn
Not if they learn to use computers. 83
You must learn to delegate as much work ... .78
We'll have to learn from experience. 30
What lessons can we learn from history? 52

Life
... taught me about life in other countries 93
We have to radically change our way of life. . .38

Patterns & Collocation

Patterns & Collocation

Patterns & Collocation

Protect

... international policies for protecting the environment. 39
... from being able to protect their industries ... 63
... but you also want to protect local people. .65
They need strict laws for their own protection. 36

Prove

I think you'd find it hard to prove. 69

Provide

When medical care is provided by the government ... 21
... can't afford to provide free health care. 21
... easier for the wealthier countries to provide aid ... 63
It's better if a sport provides an outlet for 69
... information provided by the global media. .92

Publicity

... the media gives heavy publicity to 69

Purpose

... give us all a sense of purpose. 75
... in order to find a purpose in life. 87

Put

What do you put on your strawberries? 41
Put the following jobs in the order in which ... 16
And by putting them on television, you will ... 71
... increases, so companies put up prices. 81
Try putting yourself in my shoes! 96

Qualified

We only employ qualified teachers with 30

Question

Think of ways to question advice. 23
I questioned society. 32
The police have questioned many suspects. . .36
Think of follow-up questions for 71
... training in questioning fundamentals. 93

Quick / quickly

That was quick thinking! 12
I couldn't turn quickly. 23

Race / racial

The human race may not survive much longer. 39
I came across so much racial prejudice when ... 12
... people from minority racial backgrounds ... .76
In the larger, more multi-racial cities 92

There's often more racial tension in 92

Radiation

... cancer caused by too much ultra-violet radiation. .39

Radical

... new, progressive ideas, and radical action ... 80
... if radical change was necessary 75

Rain

The rain forests are being cut down. 41
Let's save it for a rainy day. 18

Raise

I'm trying to raise money to help 18
You could raise a happy family. 87

Rate

... no noticeable difference in the murder rates. 33
The crime rate continues to increase. 36
... we could keep salaries and hourly pay rates low. 65

Reach

We could then reach our potential as full members ... 93

Ready

... we're not ready to know what's really going on. .45

Real / really

... any of my boyfriend's flirting – real or imagined! .8
I found who my real friends are. 32
... change the way you feel if you really want to. 9
What you're really saying is that 63
Not really, but my rent's too high. 89

Reason

Give reasons. 16
The reason why many women don't ... is 57
Think of various possible reasons. 32
... and reject it with reasons. 11
... or for another reason? 34
... need to take a close look at the reasons for ... 9

Reduce

What should the ... police do to reduce crime? .32
... and do very little to reduce poverty and hunger. 62
How can you reduce taxes and improve health care ... ? 77
If we reduce defence spending so much 77
... so as to reduce the trade deficit. 80

Patterns & Collocation

Patterns & Collocation

Touch
... campaign was touch and go until the very end. 78

Trade
I believe in free trade. 63
The trade deficit is getting larger. 80

Treat
... unless they are treated as equal professionals ... 96
You were expecting to be treated with great respect ... 47
I'm going to treat myself to a big dinner. 84

Treatment
Most people received poor medical treatment. 50
She needs emergency treatment. 24
If a doctor refuses to give unnecessary treatment ... 21
... have to wait longer for treatment. 21
He's responding to treatment. 23

Tree
Money doesn't grow on trees. 18
She can't see the forest for the trees. 42

Trend
What are the current economic trends ... ? 80

Turn
Take turns to be the famous person with a problem. .23
I suppose everything turned out OK in the end. 32
I was disappointed that she turned up so late. 90

UFO
There've been many sightings of UFOs. 44
... and probably even have evidence of UFOs. 45

Unanimous
We won with a unanimous vote. 78

Unfortunate
... unemployment is an unfortunate necessity? .82

Universe
We may discover the origin of the universe. . .44

Unnecessary / unnecessarily
If a doctor refuses to give unnecessary treatment ... 21
... might become very sick or die unnecessarily. 23

Until
... was touch and go until the very end. 78
... who would win until the last minute. 78

Vaguely
... who I vaguely remember from a long time ago. 94

Vary
... customs vary from country to country. 96
School fees should vary according to 30

Vice versa
... about girlfriends and not boyfriends, or vice versa. 58

View
... but they often spoil the view. 42
We have a breathtaking view of the sea. 42
A large building blocks the view. 42
... alternative points of view were fairly represented. 75
Idealists may have extreme views. 74
... influenced your view of the world? 94

Violent
... there'd be far less violent crime. 33
Violent sports ... should be banned. 69

Voice
I'm losing my voice. 23

Vote
Everybody over eighteen is entitled to vote. . .78
We won with a unanimous vote. 78
may lose a vote of no confidence. 78

Warm
... often say we are very warm-hearted. 95

Warming
I'm sure it's all because of global warming caused ... 38

Warn
When you warn me not to ask her out, it 70

Waste
It's a waste of money. 18
... are applied to health care, it leads to waste ... 21
It takes generations for nuclear waste to 41

About the Author

David Paul was born in Weymouth, UK, went to secondary school in Dorchester, and graduated with an MA in Social and Political Science from Trinity Hall, Cambridge University.

After teaching EFL in the UK, he went to teach in Hiroshima in 1980 and has been based there ever since. In 1982, he began his own language school, 'David English House', which became the largest school in the area after a few years.

Since 1981, he has written a number of best-selling course books, run teacher training courses throughout East Asia, set up franchise teacher training centers in Korea and Thailand, and been a plenary or featured speaker at many major conferences in the region.